# Adoption as a Ministry, Adoption as a Blessing

# as a Ministry, Adoption as a

MICHELLE GARDNER

Pleasant Word
A Division of WINEPRESS PUBLISHING

Printed in the United States of America

Packaged by WinePress Publishing, PO Box 428, Enumclaw, WA 98022. The views expressed or implied in this work do not necessarily reflect those of WinePress Publishing. The author(s) is ultimately responsible for the design, content and editorial accuracy of this work.

Unless otherwise noted, all Scriptures are taken from the Holy Bible, New International Version, Copyright © 1973, 1978, 1984 by the International Bible Society. Used by permission of Zondervan Publishing House. The "NIV" and "New International Version" trademarks are registered in the United States Patent and Trademark Office by International Bible Society.

Scripture references marked KJV are taken from the King James Version of the Bible.

Scripture references marked NASB are taken from the New American Standard Bible, © 1960, 1963, 1968, 1971, 1972, 1973, 1975, 1977 by The Lockman Foundation. Used by permission.

ISBN 1-57921-581-5
Library of Congress Catalog Card Number: 2003100183

*This book is dedicated to my wonderful husband, Steve,*
*for letting me follow my dreams,*
*and to*
*my beloved father, Larry Martin,*
*who was also a writer*
*and would have loved to see this book in print.*

# Table of Contents

# CHAPTER 1

## An Heir, A Spare, and A Little Princess

*G*rinning at me from the table in the teacher's room at Morrison Academy, a school for missionary children in Taiwan, my friend Julie said, "Two boys and a girl—we Chinese consider that the perfect family! You have an heir, a spare, and a little princess. Most of us wish we could have that many children, but we can't afford them."

It did seem in many ways that we had the perfect family. Our family of five had been serving in Taiwan as missionaries with CBInternational for two years, teaching at the missionary kids school and helping in a Chinese church. Steve taught third grade and I taught English classes to students who had a different first language. The missionary children were from many countries, including Finland, Korea and India. We also taught children of businessmen who came from several different countries. We enjoyed our ministry very much and had many Chinese friends in our neighborhood. It seemed the Lord was blessing our lives and giving us the satisfaction of gaining familiarity with a new culture.

Our sons Peter, age ten, and Aaron, age eight, enjoyed living in a Chinese neighborhood. What they didn't enjoy was attending Chinese school on Saturdays! Morrison Academy operated on the western system of five school days a week, so we encouraged the boys to improve their Chinese language skills by attending Chinese school with the neighbors when they had the chance. The school kindly allowed them to attend irregularly and the boys' Chinese skills soon surpassed ours.

Our daughter Susannah, age five, attended Chinese kindergarten. She was the only foreigner in the school so she attracted a great deal of attention with her curly blonde hair. Each morning I took her to school on my bicycle, riding past coolie-hatted women working in water-logged rice paddies. When I dropped Susannah off at the school gate her classmates called out, "Meigworen, Meigworen!" (American!) Susannah sighed and said, "Don't you think they should be used to me by now?" With a grin she hopped off the back of the bicycle and ran in to class.

We were beginning our third year in Taiwan in 1994 when we began hearing a great deal about abandoned girls in mainland China, primarily due to their One Child Policy. For many reasons, including the desire for security in their old age, families often desire that their one child be a son. This has resulted in many baby girls being abandoned so that families can try again to have a son. The girls usually end up in government orphanages. The Chinese government allows families from other countries to adopt the children living in orphanages, and in recent years more than 7000 Chinese children have come to the States each year. The vast majority of these children are under a year old, and most are adopted by childless couples.

As I learned more about the plight of these girls and what their future would be like if they remained in the orphanages, I became more and more preoccupied with the thought that perhaps we could adopt one child. Not a healthy baby, but an older child with medical needs who probably wouldn't have much of a chance to have a family. Steve felt that our family and ministry were thriving, and wondered if it would be wise to risk everything for a child we didn't even know.

We spent days thinking, talking and praying about it. I thought of Gentiles in Europe during World War II, many of whom risked their lives to help Jews escape the horrors of the holocaust. I had often wondered what I would have done if I'd been there—would I have valued the lives of Jewish neighbors enough to jeopardize my own family to save them? I hope I would have, but I think it's impossible to know until we're in a similar situation.

The Jews were persecuted because of their nationality and religion. Now there we were in Taiwan, just across the strait from children who were suffering just because of their gender. Of course, adopting an older child with special needs was not nearly a comparable risk to helping the Jews, but it still involved taking a stand against injustice with uncertainty about the affect on our family. At this point we didn't know anyone else who had adopted internationally or had adopted an older child. We really didn't have any idea where to start.

Steve and I decided to search Scripture and see if we could find any indication of the Lord's feelings about adoption and needy children. What we found opened our eyes to a ministry that has largely been overlooked by the body of Christ.

# CHAPTER 2

# What the Bible says about Ministering to Children who Need Families

Both the Old and New Testaments present adoption as a positive part of the Lord's plan for some lives. Moses, Samuel, Esther, and Naaman's wife's servant girl are examples of children who were raised by people other than their birth families. In each case, it is clear the Lord had a reason for the children's situations. Each of these young people had a major impact on Israel's history, and in each case this would not have happened if the children had remained with their birth families. The Lord has a plan for each life, and sometimes adoption can be part of that plan.

In the New Testament adoption is presented as a beautiful picture of what happens to believers at the moment of salvation. Ephesians 1:5,6 tells us that "In love he predestined us to be adopted as his sons through Jesus Christ, in accordance with his pleasure and will, to the praise of his glorious grace, which he has freely given us in the One he loves." Our adoption as believers is a result of the great love God has for us.

Clearly adoption was familiar to the New Testament readers, and was considered positive, or the Lord would have used a different illustration to picture our relationship with Him. He wanted believers to understand not only the permanency of the adoptive relationship, but also the love that motivates it. It is obvious that adoption is not a second best way to form a family. It is one option a family can choose, allowing them to be part of the Lord's plan for a precious child.

In James 1:27, James writes "Religion that God our Father accepts as pure and faultless is this: to look after orphans and widows in their distress and to keep oneself from being polluted by the world." There are two aspects to the religion that God accepts—one is an outward display of love and the other an inward development of holiness. Both are critical. It isn't enough simply to be a moral person, but there must be an outward expression of that inward morality manifested in caring for those who can't care for themselves.

To whom is James referring when he urges us to care for orphans? The Greek word "orphanos" is rendered "fatherless" in several translations. In John 14:18 the same word is translated "comfortless" or "orphans" when Jesus says He will not leave the disciples permanently (comfortless or as orphans) but will return to them. Ultimately He will send the Holy Spirit to remain with them as a comforter forever.

James apparently wasn't only speaking of an orphan in the strict sense of having neither father nor mother, but a child who doesn't have anyone to permanently care for him. An orphan can be any child who doesn't have a permanent family, for any reason. This includes children in foster care and institutions as well as literal orphans. There are millions of orphans worldwide. We have the opportunity to welcome some of them into our homes and church fellowships and lavish the Lord's love on them.

James tells us to look after orphans in their distress, or as some translations read, to "visit" them in their distress. The Greek word "episkeptomai" does not merely mean to go see them, but to relieve their problems. It is also used in Matthew 25:36 and 43 in reference to caring for the needs of someone sick or in prison. Not a shallow term, it implies a commitment to fully meet the needs of the person to whom we minister. James indicates that this type of commitment results from an outpouring of a heart determined to follow the Lord rather than follow the world's standards.

We were intrigued that of all the examples of true religion James could have used, he spoke of meeting the needs of those who can't meet their own.

Clearly it is every believer's responsibility to care for orphans, not just a select few. If we truly believe this, in every church there should be families ministering to "orphaned" children in a variety of ways.

There are many possibilities which will be affected by an individual's spiritual gift. A person with the gift of service might minister to children's physical needs by sending blankets to orphaned children in Sudan. Someone with the gift of prophecy might be a children's court advocate. Others might be foster parents, adopt children, or enable these ministries to happen by supporting them in various ways.

The method a family chooses to use to minister to children needing families isn't as important as the fact that we all should minister to these children in some way. The love that we lavish on these children will be both a testimony to the world and an opportunity to show our love for the Lord. Ultimately in the day of judgment "The King will reply, 'I tell you the truth, whatever you did for one of the least of these brothers of mine, you did for me.'" (Matthew 25:40).

The Lord's attitude toward children is apparent in many other passages. In Psalm 82:3 unjust judges are urged to "defend the cause of the weak and fatherless; maintain the rights of the poor and oppressed." The Lord has a special heart for those who can't care for themselves.

Matthew 19:13–15 says, "Then little children were brought to Jesus for him to place his hands on them and pray for them. But the disciples rebuked those who brought them. Jesus said, 'Let the little children come to me, and do not hinder them, for the kingdom of heaven belongs to such as these.' When he had placed his hands on them, he went on from there." Although the disciples clearly saw the children as an interruption, perhaps feeling that Jesus had more important things to do than spend His time with the little ones, Jesus Himself made it clear that He valued the children and didn't see time spent with them as a waste.

Children are seen as a blessing here, as indeed they are throughout Scriptures. Psalm 127:3–5 tells us, "Sons are a heritage from the Lord, children a reward from him. Like arrows in the hands of a warrior are sons born in one's youth. Blessed is the man whose quiver is full of them." Considering the positive attitude in Scripture toward adoption, it doesn't seem to matter how children join a family. A large family is seen as a blessing.

Too often today we don't regard children this way. The majority of families want one or two children, perhaps feeling that it is too expensive or time-consuming to have more. Yet each child is a unique creation. In Psalm 139:13–16 we see the Lord's delight in designing each one of us. "You created my inmost being; you knit me together in my mother's womb. I praise you because I am fearfully and wonderfully made; your works are wonderful, I know that full well. My frame was not hidden from you when I was made in the secret place. When I was woven together in the depths of the earth, your eyes saw my unformed body. All the days ordained for me were written in your book before one of them came to be." The Lord has a plan for each life, and children with challenges are created by Him for a purpose.

Although we can minister to orphans in many ways, as we pursued this study we came to believe more families should consider the longest ministry commitment possible—adoption. Many families could welcome another child into their homes, not out of guilt or obligation, but out of the great blessing it brings both to the child and to the family. Just as there is a spectrum of caring for orphans, so there is an ever-increasing spectrum of blessing that comes with deeper commitment and obedience to this command.

Adoption, especially of waiting children, holds challenges. The support of a church body committed to adoption as a ministry, however, can lighten many of these challenges. Nevertheless, families shouldn't begin adoption and foster care lightly, but only after earnestly seeking the Lord's direction.

The attitude with which a family approaches adoption is critical. No one, least of all a vulnerable child, wants to feel like he is being rescued. A family needs to be sure they aren't acting out of pity. However, to act out of kindness and love and the desire to share their abundant blessings with a child is certainly a proper motive.

Adopting a child and giving him a future and a hope paints a beautiful picture of what the Lord does for us in welcoming us into His family. Under Roman law an adopted son was entitled to all the privileges and rights of a biological son. In fact, we learned that in New Testament times a Roman family could disinherit a birth child, but could not disinherit an adopted child. The relationship was permanent. Christ is God's "biological" son, and believers are His sons by adoption, yet they are co-heirs according to Romans 8:17—"Now if we are children, then we are heirs—heirs of God, and co-heirs with Christ, if indeed we share in his sufferings in order that we may also share in his glory."

As we get to know our Heavenly Father and desire to become more like Him, we will love what He loves and hate what He hates. His attitude toward children will become our attitude. The more we choose to enter into this loving, caring continuum of providing for children without families, the more we will demonstrate the heart of our Father who loves children so much.

Of course, not every family can adopt a child, for various reasons. Families should, however, at least consider that the Lord might want to use them in this way. Believers' spiritual gifts will help determine their involvement in ministry to orphans. There are ample opportunities for all believers to fulfill the imperative of James 1:27.

# CHAPTER 3

## The Reluctant Father

### BY STEVE GARDNER

*Y*ou want to do *what*? That was the question that rang in my head and unfortunately came blurting out of my mouth when Michelle first mentioned the idea of adding another child to our family. Frankly, I had to agree with the Chinese that our family was perfect as it was—at least in terms of size.

When Michelle and I were in premarital counseling one of the questions that came up was about family size. I had always envisioned having two children, a girl and a boy. Michelle, on the other hand, had always dreamt of a large family. For my sake I think she limited the number to four during our counseling sessions. Ultimately we compromised and agreed that three would be the perfect number. And now here she was, going back on her promise. Michelle, of course, remembers the events of that counseling session somewhat differently and says she never agreed to limiting our family to three, but merely that that would be a starting point. In any event, here she was posing the adoption question to me.

I knew we would never have any additional biological children since shortly after Susannah's birth we found out that Michelle is a carrier for a terminal disease. None of our three biological children inherited the gene for the disorder, and we felt the Lord had been very gracious to us, perhaps because we hadn't been aware of the risk involved at the time we had our children. It seemed foolhardy to risk giving birth again. We knew the Lord could intervene and protect our future children, but we also believed that just because we were Christians we weren't immune to statistics. Since we had decided that we wouldn't have any more birth children I had assumed that our family was complete.

So now why in the world would we want to run the risk of ruining a perfectly good family? Our biological kids were just getting to the age where they were demonstrating some independence. Frankly I enjoyed the freedom this afforded us. And how would a new child with unknown issues affect our ministries in Taiwan? Another issue that was in the forefront of my thinking was how in the world we could afford such a costly endeavor. The $14,000 price tag attached to the process seemed virtually insurmountable on our missionary salary. Sure we had savings, but did I really want to empty our bank account for what I saw as a whim on Michelle's part? After all, there are millions and millions of children in the world without families. What difference could we possibly make? What difference would our little raindrop make in that vast swirl of torrential downpour?

Another issue that came to mind was the size of our house. In Taiwan houses tend to be smaller than in the States. We lived in a simple three bedroom home that was larger than most. Peter and

Aaron shared the largest room, Michelle and I the middle bedroom and Susannah had a small bedroom to herself. Where would we put another child? Then there was the issue of transportation. Because of the expense of automobiles in Taiwan we traveled by taxi. Our current situation allowed us to take one taxi wherever we went. I would sit next to the driver and Michelle and the three kids would scrunch into the backseat. What were we supposed to do, strap this new child to the roof? Or hail two taxis and double the expense every time we wanted to go someplace? Since we lived in a rural area it was hard enough to get one taxi.

Those were my initial thoughts, and the more I considered this idea the more questions arose. What issues would this new child bring into our family, especially since Michelle was talking about bringing in an older child with health issues? One of the children Michelle was considering had a hole in her heart, and the other had a cleft lip and palate. I had first hand knowledge of what a cleft palate involved since my grandmother had been born with one. She talked with a nasal tone that wasn't hard for me to understand but sometimes caused embarrassment when my friends couldn't understand her. Why in the world would Michelle want to bring a child with these kinds of health issues into our family?

And what about the child's disposition? We had been blessed with three good natured children—very compliant, never giving us more than minor disciplinary issues to deal with. What kind of emotional baggage would a child who had been abandoned at birth and raised in an institution bring to the family? Why rock a steady boat?

But it quickly became evident that this was not a passing phase in Michelle's spiritual journey. It had, in fact, become an issue whose roots had established themselves quickly in her life and were growing deeper every day. Her persistent desire to adopt was also different than other issues which had arisen during our marriage. There was a different spirit in the way she discussed this issue. Never harsh or judgmental, she simply encouraged me to seek the Lord's will through prayer and personal study. I assured her that indeed I would commit the matter to prayer and study, but that I had to be honest and let her know that I really doubted I would change my mind. To her credit, she never allowed this to become a wedge between us, nor did she allow it to dissuade her from her personal conviction.

I wanted to be true to my word, so I did spend a great deal of time praying about our future and studying Scripture about adoption. I wanted to be able to tell Michelle that I had sought the Lord and felt strongly that He was not leading in this direction. I couldn't honestly do that unless I actually did the study.

A strange thing began to happen. Quite subtly at first, and then more obviously as time went on, the issue of adoption and atrocities toward girls in China began to crop up more and more frequently in various ways. I'd pick up a magazine and there would be an article about adoption. I'd be reading the English newspaper and there would be an article about some heinous act toward children in other parts of Asia. I'd turn on the radio and hear a commentary about the situation in China. Friends from the States sent sermon tapes and again the issue of adoption was a prevalent theme. All these things began to work on my heart. It wasn't that I was completely opposed to adoption. I had just never seen it as a possibility for our immediate family.

Every time I opened my Bible it seemed like adoption and the Lord's love for children jumped out at me. The numerous times in the Old Testament that God used a form of adoption to shape children's lives became obvious. Suddenly I found myself asking a different sort of question. I no longer asked in what ways God had made it clear that adoption was not an option for our family. Instead I began to look at ways He had made it clear that it was.

About this time the Lord brought some families into our lives who had adopted their children. As I observed the Schmids and Hamptons I saw what healthy relationships they had with their children. I also realized how blessed these families were to have these precious children in their lives.

The more I prayed about it and the more I studied the more it became obvious that God was using Michelle and these other events to reshape the way I thought about what our family was to look like. Then the most marvelous revelation occurred. Adoption is a beautiful picture of what the Lord had offered to me the day I asked Christ to become my Savior. Parallels flooded over me in rapid succession. God accepted me bag and baggage with no strings attached. He opened His eternal kingdom to me, not as a slave but as a son, a joint heir with Jesus.

It became quite clear that the Lord did want us to open our home to another child. And so together and united in focus Michelle and I began the process of bringing Lee Bo into our family.

Michelle hadn't really started the process without me. Because she didn't I could be an active participant in our adoption adventure. The Lord continued to affirm our decision through numerous miraculous events throughout the adoption process.

There was a real peace that came over me and I knew we were doing the right thing. So on Michelle's birthday I gave her a travel book to China and told her I hoped it would lead us to our next child.

It made sense to add one child to our family. Little did I know that was only the beginning.

# CHAPTER 4

## Lee Bo's Story

After searching the Scriptures and learning that adoption is a beautiful picture of the Lord's relationship with believers, Steve gave me permission to do some research and see what I could find out. He still wasn't certain that the Lord was calling us to adopt. Perhaps He could use us to minister to orphans in a different way.

In 1994 the internet wasn't in common use yet, so information wasn't so freely available. I finally located a list of U.S. adoption agencies and began sending for information.

As responses arrived I was disappointed to learn that most agencies won't work with U.S. citizens living abroad. It's difficult enough to satisfy the requirements of two governments, the U.S. and the government of the child's country, and adding a third government complicates the process further. But we knew that if the Lord was truly directing us to add a Chinese child to our family He would provide the way to do it.

We also were aghast when we found out the cost of an international adoption. Agency fees, notary fees, immigration costs, donations to the child's orphanage, home study fees, and travel costs all add up. Our cost to adopt from China would be about $12,000 to $14,000. It would pretty much exhaust our life savings, and as missionaries we didn't have much extra.

One day a response arrived from another agency. The cover letter was written by a woman who had grown up in Taiwan, stating she would be eager to work with us even though we lived overseas. She enclosed a brochure that had pictures of some older waiting children. I sat nervously in my office at school holding the brochure, certain that when I opened it I would see a picture of our future daughter.

Finally I opened the cover, and to my shock saw pictures of only three girls! The other seven pictures were of boys. We hadn't even considered that the Lord might have a boy for us, so I turned my attention to the girls. One was crossed out—she had already been placed. The two remaining girls were both four years old. One had been born with a hole in her heart, and the other had a cleft lip and palate. The answer seemed obvious to me at once—living in Taiwan, I wasn't sure we would have access to the medical care a child with a heart problem would need. Steve's grandmother had a cleft palate, so that medical issue didn't seem too formidable.

I had to wait until recess, then I hurried to Steve's classroom. "Look! I think she's our daughter!" I said as I pointed to Lee Bo's picture.

## The picture of Lee Bo in the agency brochure

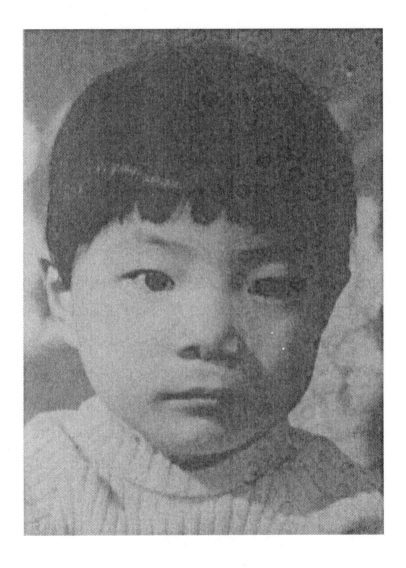

Steve looked it over carefully. "Hmm, this is interesting. We need to keep praying about it. I'm just not sure."

Disappointedly I walked back to my office. "Well, Lord, it's up to you to change one of our hearts. I don't want this whole thing to cause a problem in my relationship with Steve."

A couple of weeks later it was my 37<sup>th</sup> birthday. Steve handed me a present with a grin. When I eagerly removed the wrapping I found a surprise—a book entitled The Lonely Planet Guide to China. Looking at Steve quizzically, I opened the book to find a note that read, "With hopes that this will lead us to our fourth child."

I shrieked joyously and flung my arms around him. "Are you sure? Do you really want to do this, or do you just want me to be happy?" I asked.

"I'm really sure. The Bible seems pretty clear that we're to look after orphans and defend the cause of the weak and fatherless. This seems like the right thing for us to do. Besides, I think it will be fun to have another daughter."

The next months were busy as we gathered all the necessary paperwork. Because we were overseas Steve's father and a friend of ours, John Gordon, got all of our U.S. paperwork organized. Faxes and e-mails flew back and forth between countries as we plodded through the list of requirements.

Steve taught English to the Foreign Affairs police in Kaohsiung, and mentioned our plans to them at one of the weekly lessons. They were excited for us and indicated it should be no problem to bring Lee Bo into Taiwan. Two months later, however, one of them asked, "Where did you say your new daughter is coming from?" Steve told them, and they gasped. "She can't come into Taiwan!

We don't allow citizens of China into our country for more than a brief visit. It is simply impossible."

Because of politics between China and Taiwan visits were severely restricted. Taiwan considers themselves a separate country, and China maintains that Taiwan is a renegade province, rebelling in a similar manner to how the southern states rebelled in the U.S. Civil War. This tension threatened to jeopardize our plans.

After a lot of thought and prayer we realized there was a solution. Lee Bo couldn't come into Taiwan as a citizen of China, but she could as a citizen of America. If we took her to the States and had her get a U.S. passport the problem would be resolved.

In our extreme naiveté we thought we could request to travel to China to adopt Lee Bo right before school ended for the year. Then we could meet the rest of the family at the airport in Taiwan (Lee Bo would be allowed to land in Taiwan as long as she remained in the airport) and head to America for the summer to acquire Lee Bo's citizenship. We had no idea that the timing of adoptions is very unpredictable, depending on how long it takes for paperwork to be processed by various agencies. We just kept planning that we would travel to China near the end of the school year, and the Lord very lovingly honored our innocence and faith.

A month before the end of school we had a travel date set. Steve and I would go to China two weeks before school ended, meet Lee Bo and complete the adoption in her city. Then Steve would return to Taiwan to finish the school year and pack the family for the summer while Lee Bo and I headed to Guangzhou, a city in southern China where the U.S. embassy would process her papers for U.S. immigration.

During the process of adoption we had to decide if we wanted to change Lee Bo's name. Living in Taiwan, we all had Chinese names in addition to our American names, and we decided we would do the same for Lee Bo. We wanted her to have a name from the Bible as our other children do, so we considered various women mentioned. Steve suggested Rebekah, who married Abraham's son Isaac, because she had to leave her family and country and go to another family and country. She went willingly, and the Bible makes it clear that Isaac loved Rebekah. We wanted our new daughter, also going to a new family and country, to know that she was loved. Rebekah seemed like the perfect name.

As our excitement about meeting our new daughter grew, we found out that getting U.S. citizenship usually takes about six months. We didn't have six months to be in the States. At best we could stay only eight weeks before we needed to return to our ministries in Taiwan. We were sure there must be a faster way, but when we contacted our senators they didn't think they could do anything to expedite matters. We wrote many letters and tried every avenue we could think of, but no one seemed to be able to help. After the Lord had clearly led us so far we couldn't imagine that He wouldn't continue to work out the details. Yet the rules seemed inflexible.

Then one day my mother called us. "Guess what?" she delightedly announced. "I think I've found someone who can help you. The U.S. Immigration officer in Seattle understands your situation. He's willing to expedite things. In fact, he thinks he can process Lee Bo's citizenship in one day!"

There was such joy in our household as we were reminded again that the Lord had control of our plans. My mom came out to Taiwan to care for our other children and also to teach Steve's third grade class while Steve and I headed to China to meet our precious new daughter.

Our bags packed, our kids cared for, all the paperwork done—we sank comfortably into our seats for the first leg of our trip, Taiwan to Hong Kong. Months of dreams and preparation were finally bringing results. The stewardess came by with Chinese tea and began to pour. Suddenly I shrieked and jumped in my seat. "Oh, no!"

"What's the matter, honey?" Steve gasped, thinking I must have been scalded by hot tea.

"I just realized that I left Rebekah's plane tickets in Taiwan! I put the kids' tickets to America in my drawer, and Rebekah's tickets are there, too! What can we do?" We needed Rebekah's plane tickets from China to Hong Kong and Hong Kong to Taiwan.

Steve was flabbergasted but calm. "O.K., we'll talk to the airline when we get to Hong Kong. Don't worry. We haven't done all this for everything to fall apart now."

The airline officials were not especially helpful. They told us we could buy new tickets for Rebekah, but having just spent our life savings on adoption fees we didn't have anything left. We decided we would ask my mom to send the tickets to our hotel in China and hope they arrived in time. After all, we would be in China for two weeks so it really shouldn't be a problem.

We landed in Nanjing and were met by our translator/guide and a driver. They assured us that the next morning we would meet our new daughter. Needless to say, we didn't sleep a lot that night, wondering what the next day had in store.

On May 23, 1995, we rose early and began exploring the neighborhood, fascinated with the sights, sounds and smells of a very busy, crowded marketplace. This was our daughter's heritage. We wanted to see as much of it as we could. We were fascinated by all the bicycles we saw—they were the primary means of transportation, and they all looked alike. We still don't know how people told them apart when several dozen were parked on the sidewalk together.

Soon it was time to hurry back to the hotel. We waited with our guide, and before long a young Chinese woman walked in holding the hand of a tiny, sober waif. "That's my daughter!" my heart cried. Although by now she was five and a half years old, Lee Bo was no bigger than a three year old, and very skinny. Very bravely but without a smile she walked over to us and said, "Nee how, Mama. Nee how, Baba." (Hello, Mommy. Hello, Daddy.) I scooped her into my arms and stared and stared, hugging her as closely as I dared.

# A joyful daddy meeting his new daughter

We spent a half hour with the orphanage director, teacher and guide. I asked questions about Lee Bo's early life while Steve played and colored with her. Finally the other adults stood to leave. They issued rapid instructions to Lee Bo, no doubt instructing her to obey her new parents, and quickly left. There we were, delivery completed and parents once again. But what do you do when you're suddenly handed a five year old with whom you can't communicate well and whose world has been so sheltered until now?

We promptly took her to our room and began to get acquainted. It was obvious that Rebekah was thrilled to have parents. She was intrigued by everything we showed her. We gave her a doll—clearly she had never played with one as she vaguely held it by the hair.

As instructed, we brought clothes for Rebekah. As we took bright red pants and a colorful shirt out of our suitcase, her eyes lit up with excitement. She quickly changed into these pretty clothes and I cut the tags off and tossed them into the wastebasket. Rebekah looked at me with surprise and scampered over. Quickly she reached into the wastebasket and took out the tags. The new doll abandoned on the floor, for several minutes she played with the tags, turning them over and looking at the bright colors, feeling the rounded edges.

The next several days were filled with meetings and additional paperwork as we completed the adoption. One day was very special. Our guide took us to see the orphanage where Rebekah had spent the first five and a half years of her life. Because of recent negative publicity about Chinese orphanages foreigners were not being allowed inside. We were very eager to see the inside of the orphanage and speak with some of Rebekah's caregivers in order to have some documentation for her of her early years of life. Steve decided this was a time when he would use all of his knowledge about the Chinese culture and try to get results.

Before we left Taiwan our son Peter, who was eleven years old, had purchased some toys for us to give to the other children who were in the brochure from which we had selected Rebekah. It was hard for him to cope with the fact that we would take Rebekah away and the other children would be left behind. He bought a pretty doll for us to give to the little girl with a hole in her heart that we had considered as a possible daughter and some cars for the boys in the brochure. Additionally we had taken many other toys and warm clothes for the other children in the orphanage.

As we spoke with the orphanage director Steve mentioned how important it was to our son that we deliver the toys to the children in person. Speaking in Mandarin, Steve commented on how much we respected and admired Chinese culture. After several minutes of conversation and trying to demonstrate our good intentions, we were delighted when the director said we could see Rebekah's former bedroom and day room.

We were quickly ushered upstairs and down a dark hallway. A worker took us to a dark room filled with wooden beds. Each bed had a thin blanket folded at its foot. There were neither mattresses nor pillows in sight. The worker pointed out Rebekah's former bed to us and told us that she had shared it with the little girl with a hole in her heart.

Hastily we were led to another room, equally dark, without evidence of pictures or toys. There were several dozen children in the room, ranging in age from four to eight. Wooden tables and chairs filled the room. Each chair had a hole cut in the seat and a plastic pot underneath. The children's pants had slits in the crotch, enabling them to remain in their chairs for hours, not even leaving when they needed to go to the bathroom.

Quickly the director called three children over to us. We easily recognized them from the brochure. Steve handed the children the toys while I snapped several pictures. Suddenly Rebekah began to sob, her face scrunched in misery as tears raced down her cheeks. She couldn't explain what was wrong, so we comforted her, waved goodbye to the other children and were quickly whisked from the room. After we had the pictures developed and Rebekah spoke English she looked at the picture that showed her crying miserably. "Do you know why I was crying?" she asked. "I thought you were going to leave me there."

After a week in Zhenjiang Steve returned to Taiwan to finish the school year while Rebekah and I flew to Guangzhou to complete her adoption at the U.S. Embassy. We arrived on a Saturday and would stay at the White Swan Hotel in Guangzhou until Wednesday. I dashed to the desk of our hotel and asked if there was a package waiting for me, hoping Rebekah's tickets had arrived. Nothing—well, surely they would be there on Monday.

As we got to know each other, Rebekah's somber attitude soon turned into an eagerness to explore her new world. The hotel had a swimming pool, and, although she was timid at first, soon Rebekah was delighted to play in the water. Whenever we had free time she begged to swim, and I exalted in seeing her relax and play.

We completed the paperwork for U.S. immigration and went to our appointment on Tuesday. Unfortunately the officer had too many cases to process that day and asked if we would return the next day. I saw our file on his desk, but agreed to return later. When I arrived the next morning the officials claimed they couldn't find our file. Somehow overnight it had simply disappeared. As the officials scrambled around the room searching for the file I pulled copies of all the papers out of my bag, so grateful for the foresight Steve had in encouraging me to copy everything. The rather chagrined but grateful officials used the copies to process our case. At last it was done and we were free to leave the country.

Free to leave, but how? It was Wednesday and our flight from Taiwan to America with the rest of the family was scheduled for Sunday. We couldn't arrive in Taiwan before then since Rebekah couldn't leave the airport. Because the White Swan Hotel in which we were staying in order to complete the adoption was expensive, one of our Chinese friends in Taiwan had contacted his brother, who lived a couple of hours from our hotel, and asked him to take us to a less expensive hotel near the airport where Rebekah and I could stay until our Sunday morning flight to Hong Kong.

A good plan, but the brother was supposed to pick us up early Thursday morning and Rebekah's tickets still hadn't arrived. I checked with the desk clerk several times a day, always receiving the same response—"No package has arrived for you. We'll let you know if one does."

I had no way of contacting the brother to change our plans, nor did we have the money to continue to stay at the White Swan. In a frantic phone call Steve and I decided he would have to buy new tickets for Rebekah if they didn't arrive by 2:00 on Wednesday, at which time he had to contact the travel agent. We would worry about the cost later. The hotel mail arrived and once again I bothered the desk clerk as I asked about a package. Impatiently she checked through the pile and found nothing for us. Discouraged, we headed up to our room to let Steve know he should order the new tickets.

Rebekah decided she was a puppy and began crawling down the hallway, barking with excitement. It was fun to watch her play, and since all the people staying on our floor were families in the adoption process I knew no one would mind the noise. As we played together I suddenly realized I was hearing a different noise in the background—the phone in our room! Quickly I turned the key and ran in to answer. It was the desk clerk. "Mrs. Gardner, the postman returned. He brought a package for you. Since he already delivered our mail he should have brought it tomorrow. I don't know why he made another delivery today."

I shrieked with excitement and scared Rebekah. Grabbing her hand, we ran to the elevator. The clerk may not have known why the postman made a second delivery, but I certainly did! The Lord was once again showing us that He was directing our steps.

I needed that reassurance again early the next morning, Thursday, as Rebekah and I waited in the lobby for the arrival of our friend's brother who would take us to a less expensive hotel where we would stay until our flight early Sunday morning. I wondered how we would recognize the brother, but then realized he would recognize us!

He arrived right on time and we climbed into a car which he had rented. As a Chinese peasant he didn't own a car, nor did he know how to drive. We chatted away in my limited Chinese and his limited English and eventually stopped for lunch. While we ate the delicious fried rice, the man stared at Rebekah. Finally he said to me, "Why did you want such a lousy looking child?"

I was speechless. I looked at Rebekah, this brave, tiny little child, and wondered how we could perceive her so differently. True, she had a scar from surgery on her cleft lip, liquids frequently streamed out of her nostrils due to her unrepaired palate, and her nose was somewhat malformed, but her courage and enthusiasm as she eagerly embraced her new life were beautiful. All I could think of was I Samuel 16:7, "Man looks at the outward appearance, but the Lord looks at the heart." I tried to explain my love for Rebekah to the gentleman, but he just shook his head. Our value systems were so different.

We returned to the car and continued traveling. It seemed like we should certainly be near the airport! After awhile I said, "We probably should stay as close to the airport as possible to make it easy for Rebekah and me to leave Sunday morning."

To my dismay he replied, "I decided it will be best if you stay at my house and I'll take you to the airport on Sunday."

I panicked. I didn't know the gentleman's name, I didn't know where we were, and I spoke Mandarin Chinese, the language of northern China, not Cantonese, the language of the region we were in. I hadn't seen an American since leaving the hotel in Guangzhou. This day was not going according to my plans!

Then I remembered that he was married to an American. Surely everything would be fine once we reached his home.

Finally we arrived in his village and climbed five flights of stairs to his empty apartment. As calmly as possible I asked when his wife would be home. "Oh, she's visiting her relatives in America and will be back in two weeks," he responded.

I think I panicked more at that point than I ever had in my life. Asking the Lord for wisdom, I looked around and spotted a telephone. After receiving permission I dialed our home in Taiwan, fervently praying someone was there. Relief filled my panicked mind as Steve answered the phone. I knew I might make matters worse if I blurted out all my concerns, so I had to let Steve know about our situation without actually describing it. He quickly realized something was wrong and asked me questions I could answer with single words. He assured me I was probably safe and would contact our friend, the brother of the man in whose home I was.

Half an hour later our friend called. His brother spoke with him in rapid Cantonese, but I caught enough of the conversation to know that no one was pleased that he hadn't followed the original plan. With Steve and our friend both aware of where we were, I knew Rebekah and I would be safe, though uncomfortable.

Because he had to work, the gentleman arranged for his friends to show Rebekah and me some sights in the town the next two days. I realized that what to me was a frightening experience was to him an expression of interest and support for what we were doing. As a peasant he had very little but shared it freely with us. I tried to take the opportunity to help him learn that the Lord values each person. In a communistic society this isn't easily believed.

He got us safely to the airport on Sunday and Rebekah and I flew to Hong Kong and then on to Taiwan. Tiredly we walked into the holding room for the flight to America. Suddenly we were nearly knocked over as Peter, Aaron and Susannah ran up to hug their new sister. I caught Steve's eye and knew I could relax. He would take over now. Our precious family was together and life would never be dull.

# CHAPTER 5

## Lessons from Lee Bo

*E*ach time we've adopted the Lord has used our experiences to teach us to trust Him in new ways. Adopting Rebekah was a huge step of faith for us. We didn't know anyone who had adopted an older child or a child with physical challenges. Because we lived in Taiwan we didn't have access to books and support groups that might have given us information. We learned as we went and faced many surprises along the way.

One of the verses that helped us make our decision to adopt was Proverbs 3:27—"Do not withhold good from those to whom it is due, when it is in your power to do it." We realized that we had the power to make a difference in the life of a child. The Lord seemed to urge us to step out of our comfort zone and follow His direction.

As we encountered the numerous obstacles in Rebekah's adoption process, there were many times when we considered giving up on the whole idea. Since we were sacrificing our time and finances it seemed like things should go somewhat smoothly! But we clung to I Thessalonians 5:24—"Faithful is He who calls you, and He also will bring it to pass." The Lord wasn't going to ask us to do something and then leave us without the resources to do it.

Lessons the Lord taught us through Lee Bo:

- Step out of our comfort zone.
- Take a risk.
- Trust the Lord's faithfulness to enable us to complete the process.

## REBEKAH LEE'S THOUGHTS ABOUT HER LIFE

## Thirteen year old Rebekah at her cousin's wedding

I am Rebekah Lee Gardner and I'm thirteen years old. My parents adopted me from China when I was five and a half. I'm really glad that they adopted me. I know that my life in China wouldn't have been very good because I'm a girl and also because I was born with a cleft lip and a cleft palate. That makes it hard to talk and to eat. Now I've had six surgeries and people can hardly even see my scar.

I wonder about my birth parents. I wonder if they have a different child now and if it's a boy or a girl. My mom tells me that my birth parents were probably artistic and athletic since I am. Maybe I got those qualities from them.

Sometimes when I think about my birth mother I get really sad. I feel like I would give up every birthday present for the rest of my life if I could just meet her one time. I really want to tell her about Jesus. I feel guilty that I have such a good life and I know that I get to go to Heaven when I die because I've asked Jesus to be my Savior. I really wish I could see my birth mom in Heaven.

I know it's impossible to meet my birth mom because I was abandoned. No one can track her down. But my mom reminds me that we can pray for my birth mom. She says maybe a Chinese Christian will talk with my birth mom or maybe missionaries will talk with her and maybe she will accept the Lord. I might get to see her in Heaven.

I love my family. My big brothers sometimes really tease me but I know that's their way of showing love. My sister Susannah and I are the same age for three weeks each year. We like to say we're twins at that time, even though she is tall and blonde and I'm short with black hair. My younger sister and brother go to the same school that I do and we have a lot of fun together.

I have two friendly dogs, I get to play my clarinet in the band, and I can go swimming a lot. I really have a good life. I know the Lord has a plan for me and I want to obey Him.

Every night my family prays together and the Lord answers our prayers. I think He will answer my prayers for my birth mother.

I like to help my parents with Kingdom Kids Adoption Ministries. I try to tell other families to adopt kids and let them have a great life.

# CHAPTER 6

## Some Questions and Answers Regarding Adoption

As families and churches consider ways of ministering to children who need permanent, loving families, there are several questions that seem to come up again and again. We have examined what Scripture says on these issues and encourage families to be open to how the Lord might direct them.

### 1. Is it right to spend so much time and money on one child?

Adoption requires great resources of time and money. Sometimes people wonder if it would be a better use of funds to donate to groups that leave children in their birth countries and minister to their physical needs there.

Excellent programs, administered by groups such as World Vision and Compassion International, allow people to support a particular child on a monthly basis and ensure the child will receive an education and other necessities. We have sponsored many children in this way over the years.

Most of the children in these programs, however, are not orphans. They live with their families who, for various reasons, usually poverty, can't provide the child with the necessities of life. These worthwhile programs allow families to correspond with their sponsored child, but provide little opportunity to build values and spiritual truths into the child's heart. Of necessity communication is rather superficial.

If a family desires to meet a child's physical needs, this is an excellent way to do so. But if a family wants to build their convictions into a child's life over a period of years and hopes to eventually see the child accept Christ as her Savior, adoption is the most profound option possible. I encourage families to sponsor children, but also to consider adoption. It doesn't need to be an either—or situation. The Lord's resources are unlimited, and we can minister to children in many different ways.

The Gospels clearly show that Christ chose to spend a great deal of His time with individuals. He ministered to crowds of people, but over the three years of His ministry He invested the majority of His time in twelve men, and even more time in a more intimate group of three—Peter, James and John. Both the crowds and the individuals were important, but Jesus constantly interacted with His small group as He dealt with the large group.

Similarly, we can help relieve the misfortunes of large groups of people by contributing to various ministries that work in war-torn countries and areas where natural disasters have occurred. We can also pour ourselves into the lives of individuals by adopting one or two children and giving them a desire to reach out to others. Many people have told us that our adoptions have inspired them to adopt, so we feel like our small efforts have been multiplied.

## 2. With so many needy children in America, should we be adopting and supporting children from other countries?

Indeed there are thousands of children in America who need foster parents and permanent adoptive homes. Christian families need to consider how they can minister to these children. According to James 1:27, they are the responsibility of believers. However, we don't need to favor either domestic or international adoption. There are families who will be able to adopt domestically and others who for various reasons will adopt internationally. In the end, many children will be blessed.

Most children in the U.S. foster care system are there because they have been in abusive or neglectful situations. Often children in orphanages overseas have other issues to deal with, perhaps including physical disabilities. Each potential adoptive family needs to consider the sort of child whose needs the Lord has best equipped them to meet. Some families will feel comfortable dealing with older children and others want to start with infants. This, too, will influence the children available to a particular family.

It is interesting to read Jesus' words in Luke 4:24–27: "I tell you the truth," he continued, "no prophet is accepted in his home town. I assure you that there were many widows in Israel in Elijah's time, when the sky was shut for three and a half years and there was a severe famine throughout the land. Yet Elijah was not sent to any of them, but to a widow in Zarephath in the region of Sidon. And there were many in Israel with leprosy in the time of Elisha the prophet, yet not one of them was cleansed—only Naaman the Syrian."

The prophets didn't go to Jews in these cases. Instead, we are told that God specifically sent Elijah to a foreign widow, and circumstances specifically led a foreign military man, Naaman, to Elisha. God chose to work in the lives of these non-Jewish individuals for His own purposes. He was not obligated to work only among a specific group of people.

In a similar way, we can have a world view that is larger than just the boundaries of America. Certainly we want to love and minister to children here, but there are needs throughout the world and the Lord may direct us to a child in any country. We have no way of knowing the plans He may have for any individual child, and we may be able to be part of something wonderful, something much bigger than just our love for one child.

When I think of the millions of children around the world who need families and then consider the few children I know who have actually been welcomed into homes it is overwhelming. I wonder why these particular children were given life, a future and a hope, the opportunity for education and medical care, the love of a family and most importantly the opportunity to learn about the Lord. Why them, out of all the waiting children? All we can know is that

God chose to work in the lives of these children for His own purposes, and we are privileged to be part of His work.

As Naaman the Syrian returned to his country knowing the true God (II Kings 5:15–17), we have the opportunity to introduce children from other countries to the truth of the Gospel. My heart's desire is that my children will love the country of their birth and their countrymen so much that ultimately they will either return to their birth country to share the Gospel or will develop relationships in America with people from their birth country and share Christ with them. I pray that the investment I'm making in my children will result in spiritual fruit multiplied many times over as they become powerful testimonies of the Lord's faithfulness.

So whether a family adopts domestically or internationally, the goal is the same—to fulfill the purposes of God by providing a loving family for a child, to raise that child to love the Lord with all his heart, soul, mind and strength and to become more like our heavenly Father as we learn more about His love for children.

## 3. What about generational sin?

Exodus 34:6–7 says, "The Lord, the Lord, the compassionate and gracious God, slow to anger, abounding in love and faithfulness, maintaining love to thousands, and forgiving wickedness, rebellion and sin. Yet he does not leave the guilty unpunished; he punishes the children and their children for the sin of the fathers to the third and fourth generation." For some, this passage makes adoption a fearful thing, as a family might wonder what sort of sin problem they are bringing into their home through an adopted child.

Interestingly, there is another relationship through which we make a long term commitment to someone of whose ancestry we are not completely aware. That relationship is marriage. Rare is the individual who knows the history of several generations in his family. Most families have a black sheep or two. Yet as we approach marriage we tend to consider our beloved apart from his family, recognizing the Lord's work in his individual life.

Historically several generations of families have lived together in one home. This is still quite true in many Asian cultures, as we observed when we lived in Taiwan. It is expected that the oldest son and his wife will care for the parents, resulting in three or even four generations living together.

The environment in which a child lives affects him greatly. A child who spends his early years with an angry grandfather may struggle with an anger problem himself. A child who lives with great-grandparents who are alcoholics may have a propensity toward alcoholism. What we are exposed to on a daily basis does impact us.

I believe the generational sin issue is primarily environmental. A tendency toward certain sins is not automatically passed down genetically, though tendencies toward certain weaknesses, such as alcoholism or drug abuse, may have a genetic link. When considering the adoption of an older child, the environment out of which the child has come is a very real factor to consider. A six year old child doesn't come into a family with a blank past.

We are so blessed that we don't live in Old Testament times, but that we have the wonderful promises of the New Testament to give us hope. Jeremiah 31 gives hope of a new covenant that is to come. Verse 34 declares "I will forgive their wickedness and will remember their sins no more."

II Corinthians 3:5–8 describes the new covenant. "Not that we are competent to claim anything for ourselves, but our competence comes from God. He has made us competent as ministers of a new covenant—not of the letter but of the Spirit; for the letter kills, but the Spirit gives life. Now if the ministry that brought death, which was engraved in letters on stone, came with glory, so that the Israelites could not look steadily at the face of Moses because of its glory, fading though it was, will not the ministry of the Spirit be even more glorious? If the ministry that condemns men is glorious, how much more glorious is the ministry that brings righteousness!" The letter, the Mosaic law, killed because it couldn't give life by itself. The purpose of the law was to make men aware of sin. The grace provided by Christ gives life.

There is abundant forgiveness for sins. Although a child's environment can negatively affect her, as parents we can boldly approach the throne of grace and plead for forgiveness for events in our child's past and any long-term ramifications of them. I'm not trying to oversimplify this issue, but it would be wrong not to recognize the ability and willingness of the Lord to forgive and begin to make all things new.

# CHAPTER 7

## Mariana's Story

$\mathcal{A}$ year after Rebekah joined our family, our twelve year old son Peter was browsing through an issue of "Adoptive Families" magazine. He came to us one evening and said, "Mom and Dad, I've found a girl that I think we should adopt. She'd be a lot of help to mom and I think she would fit into our family really well." Then he showed us a picture of a gorgeous thirteen year old East Indian girl! We chuckled and assured him she was a bit too close in age to be his sister—he'd need to keep his hormones in line!

He smiled and said he was just kidding. He really wanted us to consider a little Russian girl named Marina whose picture was just below the Indian girl's. We glanced down and saw a child with the biggest smile we'd ever seen, holding two little stubs in the air where her arms should have been.

# The picture of Mariana that Peter saw in the magazine

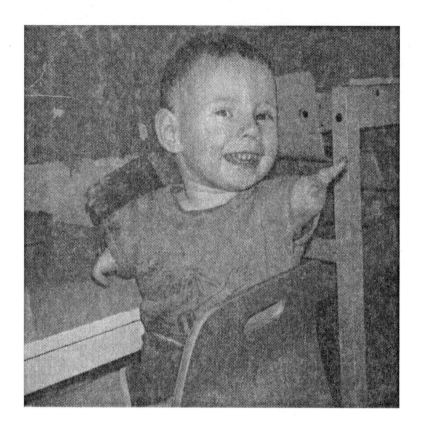

"I don't think so, Peter," Steve said. "That little girl will have a lot of challenges. Besides, our family's full with two boys and two girls."

"Well, will you just pray about it?" asked Peter. "I really think the Lord wants her in our family."

Steve and I were speechless. When your twelve year old son asks you to pray about something, we knew you probably should.

So pray we did, feeling like we were crazy even to be considering adding another child to our family, let alone a child with such serious needs. We realized that we really couldn't make an intelligent decision unless we did some research on her situation, so we contacted the adoption agency that was representing her.

They were able to give us limited information but said we had to have our home study updated to receive Marina's complete medical information. Before taking that step we contacted medical groups in the States that work with children with limb deficiencies to find out about her probable long-term prognosis. The one thing we were sure about was that if we actually considered adopting Marina we would want her to be able to live independently someday.

The medical groups were extremely positive and assured us that there was no reason Marina wouldn't be able to live independently. Without knowing her exact situation it was difficult, but they said she might be able to use prostheses and should be able to drive a car and care for herself.

With that encouragement we decided to update our home study and get the rest of her medical information. After the home study interviews I made a quick trip to the States to visit my parents. My dad was struggling with a long disabling illness and I wanted to see him while we could still have a good conversation. A package from the adoption agency arrived while I was at my parents' home. In my heart I had already decided that I wanted this beautiful little girl as my daughter. Yet having spent our life savings on adopting Rebekah we had no money for another adoption. Additionally, we knew most people would think we had really gone over the edge if we adopted again.

I tore open the package and discovered several photographs of Marina, her medical and social reports, and a three minute video-tape. Quickly I called my parents into the room and we watched the video. Three and a half year old Marina was dressed in a calf-length, fluffy blue dress and sent outside to play in the orphanage yard. Valiantly she tried to climb the rusty monkey bars, her dress getting wrapped around her feet as she hung on to the bars with her stubs. As she smiled at the camera I fell more deeply in love with her.

As I read through her medical report, however, it became apparent that Marina had several issues other than missing arms. Her birth mother was an alcoholic and there were concerns about Fetal Alcohol Syndrome. The report also said Marina was developmentally delayed.

I emailed the information to Steve in Taiwan and his response was guarded. He hated to dampen my enthusiasm but wanted us to be realistic and consider how adding such a needy child to our family would affect us all. He told me that he would look over all the information when I returned to Taiwan and we would make a decision.

It was a very special blessing to be able to share all of the information with my parents while there. Because my dad had been disabled for several years and had progressed to a wheelchair, he and my mom were able to discuss the challenges of living as and caring for a disabled person. Before I returned to Taiwan they told me their opinion. If we believed we could provide a good life for Marina and if we thought she would add joy to our lives, they thought we should go ahead and adopt her.

Not everyone felt that way. As we shared the possibility with other family members we got mixed reactions. One relative quite candidly said that it made him sick to his stomach to think about what we were considering doing to ourselves and our other children. He believed Marina would never marry or be able to support herself and would need to live with us permanently. He strongly advised us to reconsider.

Reconsider we did. We discussed every angle of the issue—how it would affect our other children, how it would affect our ministry in Taiwan, how we could possibly afford not only the adoption but also raising five children. It seemed so foolish, and yet we kept coming back to Matthew 25:40—"The King will reply, 'I tell you the truth, whatever you did for one of the least of these brothers of mine, you did for me.'" Would we miss out on this opportunity to minister to the Lord through this precious child?

Steve had to go to Thailand for two weeks to take a class. We wanted to get the decision resolved so we could have closure and go on with our lives. The kids and I already knew we wanted Marina in our family but as the breadwinner and leader of the family Steve still wasn't sure. He told me he would make his final decision while he was gone, away from our wistful glances, with time to seek the Lord in prayer. I assured him I would accept his decision as final and wouldn't plead for him to reconsider yet again.

Steve says those two weeks were some of the most difficult and yet faith building times of his life as he knew he had to make a decision. The fact the Lord allowed him two weeks away from the family to truly make the decision away from any pressure from the other family members was a blessing.

Upon his return Steve handed me a large bag and urged me to unwrap it. Inside were several small packages. The first contained a beautifully carved wooden elephant. The second contained a slightly smaller elephant. I continued opening packages and finding beautiful elephants. When they were all opened we placed all seven of them in a row. Seven? Why had Steve purchased seven? He smiled and told me they represented our family—the two of us, Peter, Aaron, Susannah, Rebekah, and Marina.

There was one other matter to consider—finances! We had very little money remaining after adopting Rebekah just a year earlier and had no idea how we would pay this time. We decided to contact the adoption agency representing Marina and ask if they would consider lowering their fees. Anxiously we emailed them and awaited their response. To our great surprise the agency offered to donate all of their fees. They agreed to make what was normally about a $16,000 expense possible for $8,000. This would include all of our expenses including travel to Russia for Steve and me. A miracle, and yet we still didn't know how we would afford the remaining $8,000.

With an odd combination of joy and anxiousness we began to gather the documents for our Russian dossier. Together we asked the Lord to close the doors if adopting Marina wasn't best for our family or for her. In international adoption there are any number of ways in which He could do this. As long as the doors remained opened we were committed to pursuing her adoption.

After making his decision to adopt, one of the next things Steve decided was that we should change Marina's name. He didn't want his daughter named after a boat dock and he wanted her to have a name from the Bible like the other children did. He decided we should name her Deborah after the only woman judge in the Old

Testament. He knew our little one would need to have a strong personality to deal with her challenges, and he wanted her to be able to understand the Lord's leading as Deborah had. We would keep Marie as her middle name for a connection to her past.

After a long wait to complete all the paperwork due to the necessity of satisfying the requirements of three countries, we finally received notice of a court date in Russia. We had managed to pay all the adoption expenses as they came up, but now it was time to pay for our airfare, a major expense of several thousand dollars. We asked the mother of one of Steve's Chinese students if she could have her travel agent arrange the rather complicated series of flights from Taiwan to Russia. Several days later her daughter handed Steve an envelope with our tickets. The bill had been paid. We owed nothing. We cried with joy.

Our church in Taiwan took an offering and other Chinese friends collected donations. Business friends who had returned to the States sent a large check. In the end Steve and I had to pay only $2000 of the total costs. We were extremely encouraged by the love and support so clearly shown to us. The Lord was definitely keeping the doors wide open.

Because my dad's health was failing rapidly, my mom wasn't able to come to Taiwan to care for our children as she had when we adopted Rebekah. Instead, she found a young woman in her church who was eager to come out to help. We agreed that Tiffany would stay with the children while we were in Russia and then help care for Deborah while I completed my teaching contract for the year.

We prepared a photo album for Deborah showing each member of our family and our home, neighborhood, school and dog and sent it off to her along with a little doll we thought she could hold. Two weeks before we left for Russia we received a video showing Deborah, now four and a half years old, looking at the photo album and saying each family member's name. We could hardly wait to hug this precious little tyke.

Our adoption agency instructed us to bring gifts for all the people who would be involved in processing the adoption. They sent a list of suggested gifts and my mom sent them from the States with Tiffany. Blenders, purses, sweaters, and cologne filled our bags.

It was April and the weather in Taiwan was getting very hot. I'd learned long ago that it wasn't worth it to put on makeup most of the year in Taiwan. When I did, as soon as I stepped outside of an air-conditioned building the makeup would begin to stream down my face. April was well into this hot and humid time. As we packed our clothes for the trip I threw in a couple of sweaters and a light jacket just in case I'd need them.

Our journey took us to Hong Kong, Thailand and Germany before we landed in Moscow. Bedraggled and tired, we exited the plane and looked for Larissa, the guide who was to meet us. The Moscow airport is dark and dreary. People in dark colored clothes scurried in all directions, some holding signs indicating they were meeting someone. There was not a sign for us. We searched the airport in vain, even approaching a few likely looking women who made eye contact with us. After an hour we realized we were on our own, not able to speak Russian and without a contingency plan. We laughed at the irony of it. At least this time Steve was with me.

The airport was chilly so we got our sweaters out of our bags. Collecting our thoughts, we searched through our paperwork for Larissa's phone number. After locating it Steve had to figure out how to make a phone call since we had no Russian money. He roamed through the airport searching for a friendly looking soul who might be willing to give him a coin. It didn't happen. Finally he approached a car rental agency and found someone who spoke enough English to understand our plight. The worker kindly allowed Steve to use the phone. Steve reached Larissa's daughter, who assured us that, although Larissa was running late, she was on her way.

As the evening cooled down further we got out our jackets and put them on. Moments later we heard a cheerful voice call our names. Larissa was heading toward us with a smile. But how had she known who we were? I glanced around at the dark colors everyone wore and then looked down at my own bright pink jacket and Steve's turquoise coat—it was pretty obvious we weren't Russian!

We spent two days in Moscow and found it all fascinating. Having grown up during the cold war, thinking of Russia as our enemy, it was very enlightening to talk with Larissa and her husband Valentin and learn that as young people they had felt the same about America. Yet now we sat around their table and realized we had many of the same dreams and hopes for our lives.

It didn't take long to realize that April in Taiwan and April in Russia are two entirely different things! Instead of humid heat, snow covered the ground and temperatures dropped into the teens at night. Steve, much wiser than I, had brought appropriate clothes. He and Larissa were shocked at the clothes I'd packed. My sweaters and light jacket did nothing to keep off the chill. Being used to wearing sandals, I hadn't even packed any socks. The first night Larissa rounded up warm clothes for me to borrow. Wearing her clothes, the next day I felt I would blend in with the crowd. Valentin laughed and said I never would unless I quit smiling. Russians tend to be a solemn group, at least out in public.

Larissa and Valentin took us driving into the countryside and we were intrigued to see many people sitting on hillsides with large rolls of thick plastic at their feet. We asked what they were doing, and Valentin told us that the people worked for a factory that manufactured the plastic. The factory had no money to pay them, so they paid them by giving them some of the product. In order to make any money the workers had to sell the plastic after working all day manufacturing it. Their lives were not easy.

Two days after our arrival in Moscow Steve and I boarded a train for Smolensk with a facilitator who spoke no English. At last we were on our way to meet Deborah. We had a four berth sleeping car and did our best to get some rest during the twelve hour trip. At four in the morning a porter knocked on the door. We had been told to expect this. It was our last opportunity to use the restroom because the toilets emptied directly onto the track and therefore weren't able to be used within two hours of a major city.

In Smolensk we met our translator, Tatiana, who had never met an American before. Her English was quite good, with a beautiful Russian lilt. Surrounded by rather dour and somber people, Tatiana was one of the few happy Russians we met.

Tatiana and Valentina helped us sort the gifts we'd brought and decide to whom we'd give each one. Then we freshened up a bit and headed to the orphanage.

As eager as we were to meet Deborah and despite all the answered prayers we'd seen, both Steve and I were quite nervous as we pulled up to the large, dark building. It was April 8, 1997. We knew that our lives were soon to be changed irrevocably. We encouraged each other to remember I John 4:18—"There is no fear in love, but perfect love casts out fear."

We entered the director's office and began distributing gifts. Soon a woman who was to represent Deborah's interests in court arrived. Hastily she called us over and told us there had been a mistake. The child's name was not Marina, it was Mariana. Somehow a typographical error years earlier had resulted in the child being called the wrong name for several years. She told us that at court we must refer to the child as Mariana. That was fine with us. We thought Mariana was a beautiful name.

In fact, Steve and I asked if it was possible just to keep her name as Mariana rather than changing it to Deborah. Certainly, the advocate told us. However, since all the paperwork had been written to say we were changing her name to Deborah, we would need to stay in Russia at least an extra week so the papers could be changed back to leave her name Mariana. Quickly we decided that we didn't care about the name enough to go through the extra work, especially since our little one didn't even know that her name was really Mariana. We would change her name to Deborah and call her Mariana or Deborah, whichever she preferred.

Having settled that, the director asked for Deborah to be brought in. Steve and I glanced at each other with weak smiles. Moments later in she walked, holding the little doll we'd sent her. She walked straight up to Steve and said, "Hello, Papa!" His heart melted on the spot.

## Mariana and her daddy—together at last

Soon the orphanage director told us they had prepared lunch for Steve, Deborah and me to eat together while we got acquainted. We were shown into a small room and each of us was given a large plate of cabbage and a bowl of soup. Left alone, we could examine Deborah's appendages and observe how she managed to feed herself and perform other tasks. It quickly became apparent that she was a very capable child. She managed a large spoon well, but the length of the handle made it difficult for it to reach her mouth. We knew that with a baby spoon or a plastic spoon she'd do great.

As we continued to hold her and eat together Deborah relaxed and began laughing so hard out of sheer excitement that she couldn't eat. She was absolutely giddy. Soon Steve and I couldn't stop laughing either. Suddenly we stopped and looked at each other as we both realized that there was absolutely nothing wrong with this child. None of the issues that had concerned us were evident. Developmental delays and fetal alcohol syndrome were not a part of this precocious child's make-up. The Lord had blessed us with a beautiful, witty little daughter. How much we would have missed if we had listened to our fears.

Soon the director and advocate asked us if we were sure we wanted to adopt Deborah. Since there was absolutely no doubt in our minds, they told us it was time to leave for our court hearing. Deborah asked to go along, but they told her she had to stay and take a nap. Right, I thought. On one of the most important days of her life I couldn't imagine she'd go to sleep.

At the court hearing the judge was somber and grim. She grilled us about why in the world we would want to adopt a physically challenged child when we already had so many other children. I tried to explain quite earnestly, but it didn't seem to make a dent in her demeanor. Then it was Steve's turn. The judge threw question after question at him, asking if he was really certain we could handle Mariana's needs. With a grin Steve said, "Of course Michelle can handle it. She's put up with me for fifteen years. She can handle anything!" The judge laughed and the tension in the room was broken. Our translator smiled and we knew the adoption would be approved.

We were escorted to office after office as the adoption papers and a new birth certificate were completed. Finally after several hours it was time to head back to the orphanage. I raced inside while Steve entered more slowly, documenting the whole thing on videotape. As I rushed into the room where Deborah and the other children were, she came over and asked, "Where's papa?" He was always the children's favorite at first.

It was with mixed emotions that we spent the next hour with the children, passing out candy and other treats. As I played with several little ones a sweet boy climbed up on my lap, snuggled in and said, "Mommy?"

"I wish I could be your mommy!" I said, knowing it was impossible to take a child without long months of paperwork having been done first. Looking deeply into his eyes I prayed that someday he too would be the chosen child.

At last it was time to leave. The children and caregivers lined up and each of them hugged Deborah goodbye. I carried Deborah out the door and she bravely left the only life she'd known.

On the train trip back to Moscow I felt subdued. We couldn't communicate with either Deborah or our facilitator and it was frustrating. Deborah wet her pants twice and we used up all the spare clothes we had brought for her. I showed her the bathroom and told her to say "Potty" but it didn't make a difference.

The first night was miserable. Deborah cried for hours, obviously overwhelmed with all the new experiences. We held and rocked her but it didn't help. We could only pray that she would soon realize how much we loved her.

Back in Moscow we were delighted to see our hostess, Larissa, again. In our absence she had made a pretty Russian dress and headdress for Deborah. It was such a kind act.

While waiting a few more days in Moscow for the United States paperwork to be completed, we decided to go to the zoo. Deborah was very excited when Larissa told her the plan. But when we approached the entrance we realized the zoo was closed. What a disappointment! Larissa tried to explain to Deborah that we would do something else fun instead, but this was the last straw for Deborah. Combined with all the other changes in her life she was fed up. She sat down in the middle of the street and absolutely refused to move.

Steve picked her up kicking and screaming and took her inside a restaurant to settle down. It was no use. The rest of the trip Deborah was stubborn and refused to cooperate with any of our plans. For a child without arms she certainly was capable of defending her territory, kicking, screaming, biting and spitting whenever we wanted her to walk somewhere with us. We began to wonder if this was a big mistake after all.

On top of that Deborah kept wetting her pants, no matter how often we showed her the toilet. We wondered why the orphanage workers hadn't told us she wasn't toilet trained. Certainly at the age of four and a half she should have been!

Finally the paperwork was done and we could head back to Taiwan. We boarded the plane and tried to fasten Deborah's seatbelt. She screamed and arched her back. Finally we got the seatbelt fastened, settled into our seats and sighed with relief. Looking Deborah in the eyes and knowing she couldn't understand a word he said, Steve smiled and said, "Honey, just wait till we get home. You're going to have to learn who's ultimately going to win this battle!"

She snarled back and deliberately kicked his orange juice off his tray and into his lap. Steve turned to me and said, "This battle may take longer than we expected!"

After several flight changes we landed exhausted in Taiwan with a sleepy little girl. Exiting the plane we saw a very welcome sight—our other four children, beaming with delight as they hugged their new sister. Steve and I looked at each other, hoping that soon she really would feel like a part of their happy group.

Deborah's feisty spirit presented many challenges over the next several weeks. As frustrating as it was, however, we soon realized that it was this same strong will for life that had enabled her to survive for four years in an environment where her value was minimal. In fact, we learned that had Deborah not been adopted she would have been placed in a home for the retarded before her fifth birthday. Observing this obviously bright child we knew that would have been the waste of a life.

Each day Deborah continued to wet her pants several times. I couldn't understand why she wouldn't tell me when she needed to go. Then one day we met a Russian speaking woman in our city in Taiwan—rather unusual. I asked her to talk with Deborah about the toileting problem. After chatting with her, the woman told me that Deborah was afraid to use the toilet. It made sense—sitting on a big toilet, without arms to support herself and without her feet touching the ground would seem scary indeed. I immediately purchased a potty chair and the problem was solved. It was the best $20 I ever spent!

As the children tried to include Deborah in their activities she struggled to find her place. Whenever something didn't go her way she kicked, spit and yelled "Duna!" Our Russian contact told us that was a rather strong word meaning "stupid". We had to teach Deb that she wasn't allowed to treat her brothers and sisters so rudely. Many battles of the will followed, and Steve and I were determined to lovingly show her she needed to obey.

Each day Deborah was more willing to let us hold and rock her and show her our love. Her tantrums became less frequent and the other children began to enjoy playing with her more.

In June Steve took Deborah to the States to process her U.S. citizenship. We marveled at how much she had changed and grown in just two months. As they left the country we were reminded again that our lives would never be dull.

# CHAPTER 8

## Lessons from Mariana

When we adopted Rebekah the main issue we dealt with was whether or not we should expand our family through adoption. When we considered adopting Deborah the main issue we struggled with was whether or not we should adopt a child with such major challenges.

Because Peter felt so strongly that the Lord was speaking to him about Deborah, Steve and I were willing to consider her adoption. We had quite a few fears about what it would mean to add her to our family, but we decided to start pursuing the adoption and to ask the Lord to close the doors if adding Deborah to our family wasn't best for either her or our family.

We clung to Jeremiah 29:11—"'I know the plans that I have for you,' declares the Lord, 'plans for welfare and not for calamity, to give you a future and a hope.'" We knew the Lord wouldn't deal with us capriciously. We believed that we could trust Him to lead through open and closed doors.

Lessons the Lord taught us through Mariana:

- Believe He can be trusted.
- Believe He can speak through a child
- Recognize how much we miss in life when we act in fear rather than in faith

## DEBORAH MARIANA'S THOUGHTS ON HER LIFE

## Deborah, age ten, as Catherine the Great in a school program

My name is Deborah Mariana Gardner and I'm ten years old. I love my life. I'm really glad that I was adopted. If I wasn't I don't think I'd be as smiley as I am.

I think that mothers should love their children, so sometimes it bothers me when I remember that my birth mother didn't take me home from the hospital when she saw that I was born without arms. I think she should have cared about me enough to take me home any way. But my parents remind me that America is different than lots of other countries. We're used to seeing people with disabilities here but in other countries they feel uncomfortable with people with disabilities. So maybe my birth mom was embarrassed about me or didn't know how to take care of me.

I was really premature, about three months, so I think it was a miracle that I lived. I think God has a plan for my life because He really took care of me. I lived in the hospital for almost a year and then when I was strong enough I went to an orphanage to live.

The people at my orphanage were nice but I couldn't stay there forever. I was supposed to go to live in a home for the retarded when I was four years old. I'm not retarded but that's just how they do it in Russia when people have physical disabilities. I don't think it's fair at all.

Since my parents were trying to get the paperwork done to adopt me I got to stay at my orphanage. Finally they came to get me when I was four and a half.

I have lots of blessings. I have so many friends and we have a lot of fun together. I go to a really good school and they always help me out when I have surgeries or break my collar bone. My brothers and sisters are usually nice but sometimes they can be pests. One of my brothers was talking about mutations one day, and now I like to call myself a cutant mutant. I like the way God made me.

I know that if I grew up in Russia I probably never would have heard about Jesus and I wouldn't have asked Him to be my Savior. I think He loved me a lot to let me come to my family here. If I had been born with long arms I'd probably still be in Russia. So sometimes things that seem hard are really good.

I wish more families would adopt children so they could have a family to love them and they could learn about Jesus.

# CHAPTER 9

## How Churches Can Minister to Adoptive Families

Adoptive families often face challenges that differ from those of other families in the church. If we truly believe the Lord calls us to love the unlovely, the weak and unfortunate, we are going to see families struggle with major issues. Should the church just say, "Well, they made their own choice," and leave a family to struggle through medical, behavioral and attachment issues alone? Or could a church consider that the entire body should be supportive of the family raising the child and help out as they could?

I would like to share some of the issues that adoptive families face that can be supported by the church body. The acceptance and help of a few friends can make a tremendous difference in successfully raising adopted children.

Of course, not all adoptive families will deal with each of these issues. However, they are common enough that the body of Christ should be aware of them and consider how they affect families in the church. Children's workers and youth workers also need to be aware of these issues so they can better understand the young people with whom they work.

Who better than followers of Christ to "defend the cause of the weak and fatherless, maintain the rights of the poor and oppressed"? (Psalm 82:3) May the Lord give you insight into how your church can encourage and support the adoption and raising of His precious children.

# GENERAL ATTITUDE OF CHURCH FAMILY TOWARD ADOPTION

Most important as we seek to develop an adoptive family ministry is the general attitude of the church family. If the body as a whole is supportive the church will be a wonderful nurturing home for adoptive families. If, however, church members don't see the value of each precious child and take the command to care for the children personally, a church can be a very critical, uncomfortable, even cruel place for adoptive families.

A couple in their late forties recently adopted a six year old boy from India. Because they married young and had their children right away, the couple's three daughters are in their early twenties and live on their own. The boy the family adopted is delayed in many ways due to environmental and medical issues. His prognosis is uncertain, but all five adults in the family eagerly love him and dote on him just the way he is. Their enthusiasm is a joy to see.

Interestingly, some members of their church have told them they were foolish to undertake this challenge. Some people feel the couple is cheating their older daughters by investing their time and money in this boy. Others feel that the couple has raised their children and should be able to take it easy now. For a family who is determined never to take it easy but to invest their lives in furthering the Kingdom of Heaven, these remarks are hurtful. A family undertaking a major ministry challenge needs support and encouragement, not criticism.

We, too, faced criticism as we prepared to adopt our sixth child. The attitude of some was that enough is enough—we'd done our part and shouldn't stretch ourselves too thin. Others felt we were cheating our three birth children of the time and money we could spend on them if we didn't have our adopted children. Interestingly, these comments have only come from those who don't know our children well and don't realize that the children actually are the ones who continue to encourage us to pursue adoptions. Having a large family has made us very intentional about spending time with each child individually.

Friends of ours took the risk of having a six year old girl placed with them who had an extremely damaging past, including having been abused sexually and through cultic rituals. They were aware of her issues and felt they could make a difference in her life. Although a few members of the church body rallied around the family and offered them support, the majority of the congregation seemed to see the child as "damaged goods". Rather than standing behind the family and supporting them, many had the attitude of "You made your own choice, now live with it." It was an extremely difficult placement and in the end the adoption was never finalized. The family has felt that a more supportive response from the church may have made the difference in enabling the placement to work out.

The general attitude of the church body toward adoption will do much to determine the degree to which families are willing to risk taking such a major step. Churches who surround adoptive families with love, acceptance and help as described in the next section will see many families obey the command to minister to orphans. Churches with critical and judgmental attitudes will probably see few families willing to minister to children in such a prolonged way.

I encourage your church to stand behind adoptive families, love them and give them support and encouragement as they minister to special children. There are many challenges involved in being an adoptive family, and the support and love of the church body can go a long way toward making adoptions successful.

## FINANCIAL ASSISTANCE

Although the government subsidizes some adoptions, most are very expensive. To invest $10,000 to $20,000 in the adoption of a child is overwhelming. Few families have such resources. Should a family even consider spending so much money on adopting a child? We realized we could either adopt our daughter from China or buy a new van for the family. In ten years the van would be old, but our daughter would have a family that loved her, surgery on her cleft lip and palate, an education and, most importantly, the opportunity to become a new creation in Christ. We decided to invest in eternity. We're still driving our clunky 18 year old car, but our daughter is healthy, learning, and an enthusiastic follower of the Lord.

Even with careful planning, families often find it difficult to come up with the finances necessary to complete an adoption.

Additionally, many families feel that adding another child to their home would create too many expenses. We need to see children as blessings rather than liabilities. For larger families, adding one more child doesn't create a lot of expense on a monthly basis, especially if the child is in school or the mother isn't working.

If a church body truly understands their responsibility to provide families for children, they can give financial assistance to adopting families. Every support possible should be given to families willing to raise and love needy children. A church could include help of this type in their yearly budget. They could take a special quarterly offering for an adoption assistance fund. Members of the church could individually support adoptive families in the congregation.

Sometimes a family can be enabled to adopt simply by loaning them the necessary funds. The federal government currently offers a $10,000 tax credit to help cover the expenses of adoption. This credit can be spread out over five years if a family's tax liability is less than $10,000. Unfortunately, the tax credit can only be used after the adoption is finalized, and therefore the money must be available up-front. A no-interest or low-interest loan by a church member, with an agreement that it would be repaid when the tax credit was received, would be a wonderful way to help finance adoption. A church could possibly set up an account for loans of this nature, which would be self-perpetuating as the loans were repaid as tax credits were received.

Our own organization, Kingdom Kids Adoption Ministries, believes it is tremendously valuable to have friends and family members involved in the adoption process. As pre-adoptive families let their friends know about their plans, we hope the friends will not only contribute financially but also begin to pray for the family and their waiting child. All of this results in donors realizing they played a significant role in the adoption. We challenge them to continue to pray for the family and child for years to come.

Gifts given to finance adoptions through Kingdom Kids Adoption Ministries are tax-deductible. We help families raise funds for adoption and we also provide grants to families adopting children with special needs. There are other organizations that can also be of help. Because of the clear Scriptural teaching on caring for needy children, financial assistance to adoptive families seems highly appropriate.

## "THE WAIT"

Pregnancy is a wonderful time of dreaming about the future, learning to love the little one carried inside, and sharing experiences with other women. Even the inevitable pains and discomfort seem somehow easier when the experiences are shared. Most people, when seeing a pregnant woman, feel comfortable striking up a conversation about when the baby is due, whether it is a boy or a girl, and how the mother is feeling. It's a special time.

The wait for an adoption is similar to a pregnancy but, in my opinion, much, much more difficult. Having been through three pregnancies and three adoptions, I'd take the physical discomfort of a pregnancy any day over the emotional stress of the adoption wait. A pregnancy has an expected due date. An adoption wait can go on for months or even years. When I was pregnant and wondered how my baby was doing, I'd poke my enlarged belly until I felt my baby move, which I took as assurance that he was just fine! When I was waiting to meet my adopted-child-to-be, I'd stare and stare at her picture and wonder if she had a cold, if she was getting enough to eat, if anyone was tucking her into bed at night. I wondered if she'd been told that she had a family who loved her and was working as hard as possible to bring her home. When I was pregnant I wondered how soon my child would sleep through the night. While waiting to adopt a frail child from a threadbare orphanage I wondered if my child would live to sleep through the nights until she was in our home.

The camaraderie between pregnant women is fun to watch and a special group in which to participate. It doesn't end after the child is born, either—women enjoy telling their pregnancy stories the rest of their lives! But because few women adopt, it's difficult to have anyone with whom to share excitement, cry over disappointment, and discuss every little detail.

A church body can help by being aware that when a family is waiting for the child they plan to adopt it is a very emotional time. Families are given pictures and other information about the child, sometimes even a video, and the child becomes part of their family in their minds and hearts long before any paperwork makes it legal. It is a very surreal feeling to love and long for a child who is states or worlds away. It helps when people express an interest in the status of the adoption. Even more helpful is knowing that people are praying for all the details involved.

Simple awareness that the adoption wait is stressful and that adoptive parents-to-be would enjoy talking about it as much as pregnant couples do can go a long way toward making the wait easier.

# HELP DURING ADOPTION TRIP

Most families adopting internationally need to travel for at least one to two weeks to their child's country. Many families adopting domestically also need to travel. Often families don't have a lot of warning as to when they will need to make the trip. Making arrangements for children and pets left behind can be challenging.

Knowing that everything at home is in good hands enables the adoptive parents to relax and invest their emotional energy in meeting their new child and getting through the necessary legal hurdles. We had friends and family rally around us when we traveled for our adoptions. People pitched in on so many levels—some drove our children to music lessons, others provided meals, one let us send faxes to his place of work. My mother even substituted for my husband at the Christian school where he taught. Knowing our children, pets and responsibilities were well cared for enabled us to focus on our new child and help her begin to bond with us.

Perhaps the Women's Ministries group in a church body could arrange for help with children and meals while the parents are away. Sunday School or Wednesday night teachers might see if parents of class members could help out. It is wonderful when other families begin to feel they have a part in the ministry of adoption by helping the family in practical ways.

# CHILDCARE ASSISTANCE

After the family has settled in, there are often childcare issues involved. Although many mothers stay at home, others need to work at least part-time, and more and more single women are adopting as well. Sometimes mothers must work to repay loans required to complete the adoption. In any case, if a church considers the adopted child as a ministry of their body, perhaps they can provide necessary child care. A stay-at-home mom might care for the child along with her own children. A woman whose children have grown might enjoy watching the child. Each church needs to consider the extent to which they will support the adopted child and family.

## BEING A SPECIAL FRIEND TO A CHILD

Over the years several people have developed special relationships with various ones of our children. We are so grateful for friends who are willing to do this. In a large family it can be challenging to meet the needs of each child, and a special church friend can be a tremendous help.

Our daughter Deborah was born with short stubs rather than arms. The stubs come about halfway to where a normal elbow would be, and each stub has a single digit. In order to allow her to use her short arms as well as possible, most of Deborah's clothes need to have the sleeves modified. In the past I whacked off most of the sleeve and sewed a new hem—acceptable but not beautiful. This year a woman in our church has taken on Deborah's wardrobe as her project, with wonderful results. She is an excellent seamstress and finishes the sleeves with ribbing, making each shirt or dress look like it was originally made with these beautiful little sleeves. This woman has also purchased some clothing for Deborah in which the sleeves were already suitable.

We have been so grateful for our friend's interest in Deborah. Not only does Deborah look better dressed, but she also appreciates the attention. It's important for children to know that people other than their immediate family are rooting for them, and this woman has made a big difference in Deborah's life.

Our other children have had people take individual interest in them through the years as well. We explained to our children years ago that we have too many people in the family to try to ensure that everything is "even", but that in the end things tend to even out. The kids understand this and none of them has ever expressed jealousy when a sibling was given a special treat by a friend. Sometimes people hesitate to give something to just one child, concerned the others will feel left out, but we always tell people that we're grateful for their interest in one child. We know that if people feel they have to do something for all the children if they want to do something for one child, none of the children will ever get a special treat!

Church members who are older or won't adopt for some reason can have a major influence on a child's life by being a special friend and helping out in various areas, thereby sharing in the blessings of adoptive ministry. People shouldn't hesitate to ask families if there is a way they could be involved. If the family doesn't have ideas, friends can think of a way they'd like to help and suggest it to the family.

## SENSITIVITY TO RACIAL ISSUES

A biracial two year old is adorable. So is a little Chinese child. Churches rightfully give these children plenty of attention and love. But what happens when these little ones reach adolescence? Do church members feel comfortable with interracial dating and marriage? If we truly believe we are to provide homes for needy children, are we ready to embrace these children in every area of our lives?

Most adoptive families realize the importance of enabling their children of different ethnic backgrounds to spend time with others of their ethnic group. This is not always easy to do, however. Small towns normally don't have a lot of minorities, and even larger cities may not have members of a particular ethnic group. Friends of ours with adopted Mexican Indian children strongly feel the need for more non-Caucasian people in their children's lives. Although they live in a large city, they have a difficult time intentionally developing relationships with people of their children's ethnicity simply because they haven't met very many.

Because we are multi-faceted, however, even if a child gets acquainted with people of a similar racial heritage they may have very little in common. The adopted child is part of a church body and religious tradition that may be quite different than that normally embraced by his or her ethnic group. The adopted child is probably also part of a middle class family. Unfortunately, this can sometimes make her different from others of the same ethnic group.

Sometimes adopted children feel like they don't really have any place where they fit in. They feel different in their own family, and they feel different among people of their racial heritage. Many adoption agencies now provide culture camps during which children can meet other adopted children of the same racial heritage, and it is among this group that some children feel the most comfortable. Other adopted children don't seem to struggle with racial issues very much. Each family needs to be sensitive to its own child.

This affects the church in several ways. Well-meaning friends can expect a child to be able to speak a language he or she never learned or forgot long ago. Stereotypes of different nationalities can cause us to have certain expectations of children, even though their talents and personalities may have been influenced more by their adoptive family than by their race. It shouldn't be assumed that two adopted Chinese girls in a congregation would be best friends—their personalities may be vastly different.

Dating is one of the biggest issues in this area. Some churches feel that interracial dating is inappropriate. Whatever an individual's beliefs, the minority young person who has been welcomed by the church as a child needs to continue to be loved and accepted throughout adolescence.

A young minority woman we know was raised as an adopted child in an all-white small town. She was very accepted throughout childhood, and as a teenager began to date some of the Caucasian young men in the town. Eventually she was engaged to one of them. However, his parents gave their son an ultimatum: if he married her, they would disown him. Not surprisingly, it wasn't long before he called off the engagement. This was very difficult for our friend and she faced a major struggle of wondering where she fit into society.

Not every family will feel comfortable with interracial dating, but church families do need to consider how they can continue to show a minority child that he is accepted during the adolescent years.

# SENSITIVITY TO ATTACHMENT ISSUES

Attachment disorders are becoming better understood as more children who have spent years in institutions are being adopted. These disorders vary. Some children who haven't had a consistent caregiver or other consistent adult in their lives learn that they must care for themselves and believe that they can't trust anyone. When these children eventually have parents it is difficult, or in some cases nearly impossible, for them to learn to trust their parents and realize they can allow themselves to be children and let someone else be the adult and parent. These children can be charming to adults other than their parents, since they don't have to allow these adults to parent them.

Other children respond in almost the opposite way and, rather than refusing to trust anyone, want to be close to every adult. Our daughter Rebekah fit this description. Because we were missionaries in Taiwan at the time of her adoption, she wasn't around very many Caucasians. The majority of Caucasians she met were also missionaries who were very kind and loving to her. Rebekah responded like a bucket with a hole in the bottom—no matter how much love and attention she got, she demanded and sought more. Since everyone was so kind to her, she happily sought affection from all the missionaries. We knew she loved us, but she also loved the others around us and we often felt that she would happily go home with any of them. We loved her and met her needs, but she felt she could get the same response from our friends.

We wanted to help Rebekah, who had never lived in a family, to understand the commitment and appropriate affection between family members. The time came when we had to ask our missionary community not to hug her or hold her or show physical affection in any way. Rebekah needed to learn boundaries and that we could show affection among family members in a way not appropriate with those outside our family.

This was difficult, since in a church body people love each other's children and in many ways a church fellowship is like an extended family. Some friends had a difficult time understanding why we asked them not to touch Rebekah. However, most people supported our request and over a period of several months Rebekah began to bond more closely with our family than with other families in the missionary community. Now she is very bonded to us and we have been able to allow friends to express appropriate physical affection to her.

Church members need to be aware of both types of attachment disorders and respect a family's requests for appropriate affection toward their adopted child. It's difficult not to hug and hold a child who obviously needs and thrives on attention, but we need to keep the child's long-term emotional health in view. Attachment disorder is complex. Numerous books and articles have been written on attachment disorder and can be consulted for further information. The important point to remember is that the problem exists and church members need to trust the parents of an adopted child if they request sensitivity to this problem.

## DEDICATING CHILDREN TO THE LORD

Most evangelical churches provide the opportunity for parents to dedicate their babies to the Lord, indicating the parents' desire to raise their child to love the Lord and follow Him. When families adopt older children, churches need to provide them with a similar opportunity.

We dedicated one of our adopted daughters to the Lord when she was five years old, and one when she was six. Our son was dedicated to the Lord when he was nine. Our church was very willing to help us in this way. In one situation our daughter was included with young babies being dedicated, and in the other situation our daughter was the only child being dedicated. The second time was very special. The pastor called the whole family up and in effect dedicated all six of us to raising Deborah to love the Lord.

A church needs to be aware that it is not only appropriate but responsible to encourage parents to dedicate older adopted children to the Lord.

## SHOWERS OR WELCOME PARTIES

In many churches women give showers to welcome new babies. This is a huge help in providing clothes and other items a family needs for their new child. It also is an affirmation that the church is excited about the new child. When families adopt older children, however, there often isn't a shower or other special welcoming event. Yet most families need clothing and other items for their older child.

There are many special ways of acknowledging the excitement a church feels about a new child, regardless of age, in the church body. Depending on circumstances the church might choose to give a shower before the child arrives, if the family needs items immediately. If the family prefers to wait until after the child's arrival, a party for entire families might be appropriate. Perhaps families with children who will be in the new child's Sunday School class might host a welcome event.

Acknowledging the new child's arrival in some special way helps the child's family feel he is not only welcomed but that the church is excited to have him.

# MODIFICATIONS AND HELP FOR PHYSICALLY CHALLENGED CHILDREN

If we are truly pro-life and believe that every life is of value, we need to be prepared to modify our church facility so that it is accessible to those with physical needs. Some of this is now mandated by the federal government in relation to the Americans with Disabilities Act, but other modifications should be done, not to meet government requirements, but to make our church facility a welcome haven for all.

The issue of meeting the needs of the physically handicapped is larger than a simple adoption issue, but it does relate to adoption. Who better than believers to care for some of the most vulnerable of the Lord's children?

As a church body observes a family with a physically challenged child attending regularly, they could meet with the family to see if they intend to make the church their home. If so, they can discuss how to make the facility as accessible as possible for the child. Most facilities are now accessible for people in wheelchairs. There are many other useful modifications that will only be discovered in conversation with an individual family.

Our daughter Deborah needs a dressing stick and a hook attached to the wall to enable her to use a restroom independently.

This is a relatively easy modification that our church has made for her.

Although she is becoming more independent, Deborah still normally requires someone to help with certain aspects of dressing, such as zipping pants or pulling up tights. Because of the very real risk of child abuse even in churches, we have been hesitant to allow her to use the restroom with people we don't know. Instead, we have asked a couple of young women who work in the children's program to be available to assist Deborah. She approaches one of them when she needs to use the restroom. She does as much as she can independently, and they help her with the rest. By having only certain people assist her we are confident that she will be cared for and safe.

Public schools are required by law to make modifications for children with physical limitations. Should our churches do any less?

## MODIFICATIONS FOR MENTALLY CHALLENGED AND LEARNING DISABLED CHILDREN

Due to prenatal exposure to drugs and alcohol and other reasons, a number of children in our churches have learning disabilities or are slow learners. It's important to make them feel comfortable in the children's programs. Sometimes this will require a higher ratio of adults to children than we normally would expect. It also may require that written materials be adapted or that the child have an adult to help him work through the materials. Lots of review and focusing on one main point each day will help these children learn along with their classmates.

A family we know has a teenage son they adopted as an infant. He has a number of learning challenges due to prenatal exposure to toxic substances. The parents have worked hard with him and he has made great progress. However, because his disabilities aren't visible, his parents sometimes feel that church members consider his struggles to be the result of poor parenting on their part, rather than recognizing that he is a challenged child who is really doing the best that he can.

We need to consider what is appropriate information to share with children's and youth workers. Families don't necessarily want everyone knowing their child's history and issues, but in some cases understanding the cause of a child's inconsistent behavior can help workers be more patient and creative in dealing with the child.

# RESPITE CARE FOR HIGH NEEDS CHILDREN

As we open our hearts to minister to children, the Lord will lead some families to provide homes for children with very intense needs. These children can have extreme physical difficulties, anger management problems, very low mental capacity, and other issues. Although the adoptive or foster parents love these children and are willing to pour their lives into them, there will be times when they need a break.

One of the greatest gifts the body of Christ can give to a family dealing with a high needs child is the gift of time away. To enable the child to function as well as possible, it is often best to have someone come into the home to care for the child there, in his familiar environment. The parents can leave for the evening or the weekend and know that their child will be cared for by someone who loves the family.

Alternatively, the child could be taken to another home for an evening or weekend to give her parents a break. This is a tremendous service a church family can provide to families who face a great deal of stress on a daily basis.

My mother-in-law has adopted three of her grandchildren. One of them struggles with ADHD and behaves very unpredictably, with emotional highs and lows. Raising three children while in their seventies is challenge enough for my mother-in-law and her husband, but the additional stress of this child's difficulties adds strain to parenting this second time around. Yet in the fourteen years they have been raising these children, no one from their church has ever offered to care for all three children, even for an evening. A break from their responsibilities so they can spend some time together would enable my in-laws to have renewed energy for their daily tasks. Giving parents a break is a valuable ministry a church family can undertake.

## ADOPTIVE FAMILY SUPPORT GROUP

As more families welcome adopted and foster children, it is appropriate to provide a support group for them in which they can deal with unique issues. We have recently begun such a group in our city and it has proven to be of immense value. One woman commented that she had never had anyone to talk with about these issues before.

A church might set up a time for a planning meeting and invite everyone they know who has adopted or is thinking of doing so. Churches might band together to create a support group. Perhaps one family might organize and advertise the group.

Not every adoptive family will feel the need to participate in such a group. Some children don't struggle with adoption issues as much as other children. However, knowing that such a support group is available if they should ever desire to participate is a reassuring feeling.

As church bodies become more committed to the idea of adoption as a ministry, there are certainly other ways they will discover to reach out to adoptive families. Most important is to recognize the value of each life and support families in their choices.

# CHAPTER 10

## Abhilash's Story

A year after we adopted Deborah we returned to the United States to live. Originally we settled near my parents so that we could help care for my dad who was in the last months of his life. After he died Steve was offered a pastoral position on the other side of the state. Accepting it would mean taking a salary reduction from Steve's teaching job. Thinking that we might want to adopt again in the future and knowing that adoptive families need to earn a certain percentage at least of the federal poverty level, Steve encouraged me to contact an adoption agency and verify that his new salary wouldn't be so low that it would preclude our considering another adoption someday.

A quick call to an agency assured us that the proposed pastoral salary would be sufficient to qualify for another adoption. As I was about to hang up the woman asked what type of child we were considering adopting. I really didn't know because we were talking about something that was just theoretical at that point, but mentioned that we probably would want an Asian child, so that

Rebekah wouldn't be the only non-Caucasian in the family, and would be interested in a child with limb deficiencies. The woman told me that she had just met a delightful little girl in Thailand with malformed hands and feet and wondered if we would be interested in her.

We really weren't considering starting the adoption process again so soon, but decided to look at the girl's videotape. When it arrived we fell in love with three year old Pearl whose smile lit up the room. "Well, let's go for it!" said Steve, much to my surprise.

The one glitch was that the adoption agency was concerned that Thailand might not let our family adopt Pearl due to the size of our family. Many countries prefer that children are placed in small families. The agency said they would contact Thailand and find out if it was a possibility before we went to the trouble of preparing all the paperwork.

Eagerly we awaited word of their decision as we prepared to move across the state. After several weeks we learned the verdict—not only were they concerned about the size of our family, but they also didn't want to place a physically challenged child in a family that already had another physically challenged child. A different family would have to be found for Pearl.

What a disappointment! We had thought that Pearl and Deborah would be a great encouragement to each other and we had met many doctors who could help with Pearl's challenges. But we also had approached this possible adoption as we had all the others, asking the Lord to shut the doors if this wasn't best for the child or for our family. As disappointed as we were, we had to admit that a negative answer from the government was a pretty definite closed door and an answer to our prayer, although not the one we wanted.

Now, however, we were emotionally prepared for another adoption and decided to contact the agency through which we had adopted Deborah to see if they could help us. Steve thought we should find out about a boy, to even out the family.

## STEVE'S COMMENTS

*When it didn't work out with Pearl I thought we should consider a boy. Michelle could hardly believe what she was hearing. I had moved from being what I considered the ultimate reluctant father all the way to the other end of the pendulum swing where I was now encouraging Michelle to consider another child. It didn't take much encouragement in terms of considering adoption, just a lot of effort to assure her I really wasn't joking!*

*It made perfect sense in my mind. When we were in premarital counseling we had discussed our ideal family size. I had said two children and Michelle had said four. I was under the impression that we had compromised on three, but in reality it was a simple matter of addition. By adopting one more we would have my two and her four! I jokingly say I'm still trying to decide which two are mine and which four are hers. It varies from day to day depending on who has gotten into the most mischief. But the reality of the situation is they are all mine. I'll be very surprised if these six are the end of the road for us as a family. Maybe we really will multiply my two and Michelle's four. Yeah, I think I could handle eight kids!*

The agency encouraged us to consider adopting from India. I couldn't believe it. I had long been intrigued with the culture and history of India and desired to bring one of their beautiful children into our home. However, I had thought it wasn't possible since India typically requires that adoptive families have no more than two children in their home. Our agency assured us that exceptions are often made for older children or those with physical challenges. They sent an inquiry to India and this time the government's answer was encouraging. They were willing to tentatively approve our family for a special needs child.

The agency told us that as soon as we had the paperwork ready for our homestudy they would send information about a prospective boy. We worked fast and soon the caseworker brought a file.

"Let's go over a few questions," she said, "and then I'll tell you about two boys and you can choose the one you think would fit into your family best."

Two boys! We had no idea that we would have to make a choice. Maybe it would be totally obvious which child should be ours. But when she shared the information we didn't have a clue about what to do. One of the boys, Abhilash, was nine years old and almost totally blind. The other one, Ganesh, was six years old, microcephalic and developmentally delayed. Their pictures were adorable and we would have loved to take them both. But Indian law won't allow families to adopt two unrelated children at the same time. We would have to make a choice.

I was haunted at night as I realized what a serious decision we had to make. One of the boys would get a family that loved him, access to good medical care, an education, a church family and the opportunity to learn about the Lord. Because of the severity of their challenges, the other boy would likely remain institutionalized. How could we possibly choose?

One day a peace filled me as I realized that we weren't the only family that would love to raise one of the boys. We just needed to find an interested family. I began talking with everyone I knew about the children, showing their pictures and looking for signs of interest. Although people were sympathetic to our dilemma, no one really seemed to care about making a home for one of the boys. We had to make a choice soon.

Stopping by the church office one day, I told my story to yet another willing listener. Audry, the church secretary, whose three daughters were raised and on their own, said that perhaps she and her husband could adopt one of the boys. I was shocked. It would require a total lifestyle change for them. Yet she continued to express interest.

Hastily calling her husband, Jim, we decided to go out to lunch at an Indian restaurant and discuss the idea. Our husbands joined us and we shared the information. Jim couldn't believe that Audry was seriously considering the idea. Why would they want to do something so drastic?

Over the next few weeks it became apparent to Jim that the Lord had prepared them for this through several mission trips to Romania and time in orphanages there. It wasn't long until he told Audry she'd soon be the mother of a little boy. The question was, which boy was theirs and which was ours?

As we prayed it soon became apparent that Jim and Audry's hearts had been captured by Ganesh, the six year old boy, and our hearts were drawn toward Abhilash. With delight at seeing the Lord's hand at work, both families began the paperwork process.

## The first picture the agency sent us of Abhilash

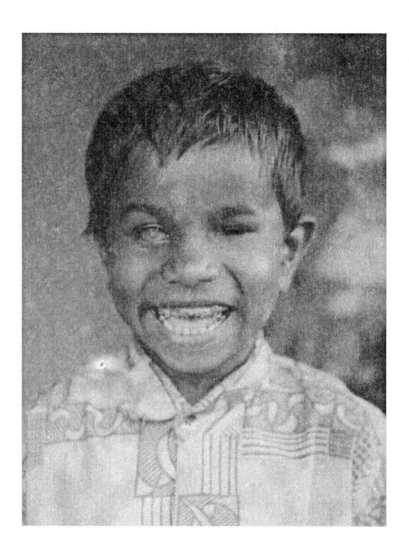

Our last remaining obstacle was finances. Before we even considered another adoption we had verified financial resources. However, now that it looked like we were actually going ahead the

money we had expected no longer appeared to be available. Now that we actually knew about Abhilash we didn't want to give up on adding him to the family.

The idea of adopting a nine year old blind child was, I admit, rather overwhelming. Abhilash had lived with his birthmother until he was about six years old. Apparently she was very committed to her young son, but because of his visual impairment and her own failing health she had turned him over to the care of an orphanage. Abhilash was missing one eye completely and had very limited vision in the other eye. A very sweet child, he didn't have much of a future in India. Schooling and job opportunities simply wouldn't be available to him.

The agency sent us a video that showed Abhilash flying a kite and writing the alphabet on a chalkboard. With his face right next to the board he carefully formed each letter. His persistence and obvious cheerfulness encouraged us that he would be able to make a good transition to life in America.

Because of his age and physical challenges India agreed to lower the fees for the adoption. We still needed to come up with several thousand dollars, however. Our past experiences had shown us that when the Lord calls a family to a ministry He will provide the necessary resources.

We realized that a number of our friends and family members were interested in Abhilash and might be willing to help make his adoption possible. We set up a non-profit foundation to which people could contribute and receive a tax deduction. Then we sent letters to everyone we knew, letting them know about Abhilash and our plans.

Within a couple of weeks we began to receive responses. It was touching and humbling to hear from friends and receive donations for Abhilash. Some friends sent $10. Others sent $1000. Many families made this their Christmas project and encouraged each family member to contribute. Others, who couldn't help financially, assured us of their prayers. Within three months we had received over $8000 for the adoption. This was enough to cover everything except the travel.

Amazingly, shortly afterwards we heard from the same Chinese friend who had paid for our flight to Russia to adopt Deborah. She wanted to help with Abhilash' adoption and sent several thousand dollars. Her donation not only paid for our travel but also allowed us to help Jim and Audry with their adoption expenses. We were so grateful for her generosity.

As we planned to add Abhilash to the family we considered what was best to do about his name. We think it encourages our children to be named after biblical role models whose lives can challenge them. I very much wanted to name a son after John the Baptist, whose statement "He must increase, and I must decrease" has made a major impact on my life. Because of his severely limited vision it also seemed like it would be a good idea for Abhilash to have a short name that he could write easily. Yet we weren't certain if it was wise to change the name of a nine year old. His identity was undoubtedly wrapped up in his name.

As a way of helping with the transition to a new life we prepared a scrapbook for Abhilash with lots of pictures and letters from each family member. As part of my letter I mentioned that we thought he might like a short name that would be easy for him to write. I told him we were thinking of the name John and said we could talk about it when we met.

Teri Bell, a representative from the adoption agency, visited Abhilash's orphanage and delivered the scrapbook. Someone read the letters to him, translating them into his Indian language. Teri told us that within a couple of days Abhilash walked up to her and said, in halting English, "My name is John. I have two brothers and three sisters." He was very eager to join his new family and liked the idea of a new name to go along with his new life.

Knowing he was so eager for our arrival made the days of waiting seem so slow. Finally the last of the paperwork was approved and Steve and I were on our way for yet another adventure.

India doesn't require that adoptive families travel to pick up their new children. Escorts are allowed to bring the children to their new home. We knew it would be less expensive to have John escorted but felt that due to his vision and his age we should meet him in his comfort zone, and thanks to the generosity of our Chinese friend this was possible.

Friends stayed with the other children while Steve and I traveled. On June 13, 2001 we landed in Cuttack, Orissa state, India. A social worker from the orphanage met us and took us to our hotel. We quickly freshened up and headed to the orphanage.

I can't deny once again feeling some anxiety as we anticipated meeting yet another new child. A nine year old can have strong opinions. What if he didn't like us? What if we didn't like him? I told Steve about my concerns and he laughingly reminded me that there are times when we don't like one or another of the other children, but we always feel love and commitment to them. With that assurance we stood at the end of a garden path and awaited the arrival of our new son.

## Happy mommy, nervous son, at their first meeting

What do you do when you first meet your nine year old son? Because his English was quite limited we knew we wouldn't be able to converse much, so I brought a little balsa wood airplane. John walked down the path, wearing a shirt we had sent him and grinning from ear to ear. He held out his hand and said, "Hello, Papa. Hello, Mama." His beautiful smile and brave spirit broke through my concerns. While I videotaped Steve and John assembled the airplane and flew it until it eventually broke.

As we spent the afternoon exploring the orphanage, one little boy, Pupunu, followed us all afternoon. A beautiful little five year old, he slept in the same room and sometimes the same bed with John. They were great friends, almost like brothers. Pupunu was very upset that we were taking his best friend away. Tears and anger alternated in his reaction to us. I knelt beside Pupunu and told him that I would try to find a mommy for him.

## Abhilash, Steve, and Pupunu at Basundhara

Later Saila, the orphanage director, told me it would be very difficult for me to fulfill my promise to Pupunu. He has a terminal blood disorder, Thalassemia Major, requiring frequent blood transfusions and other medical interventions. His life expectancy was about twelve years old, making it very difficult to find a family for him. Steve and I asked if it would be possible for us to adopt him, but Saila's answer wasn't encouraging. It would probably take two years to finalize John's adoption and complete the paperwork for Pupunu. He needed a family in America much sooner than that. I promised Saila that I would do my best to find a special family for this special little boy.

After spending a few hours seeing John's bedroom and school-room and meeting his friends we decided to return to the hotel for the night. We asked John if he would like to stay at the orphanage and have us return in the morning or if he wanted to go with us then. Without any hesitation he assured us he was ready to go with us.

That first night at the hotel was the beginning of a new world for John. We went to the dining hall for dinner and allowed him to choose, with the waiter's help, from anything on the menu. Curried mutton on rice was his favorite. We had been told to expect quite different table manners, so weren't entirely surprised when John began to eat the meal with his right hand rather than with silverware. Knowing he was facing so many changes at once we decided not to make him change yet.

Up in the room Steve got a bath ready for John and motioned for him to hop in. He looked at Steve in confusion but eventually complied. We soon realized this was John's first bath and certainly his first experience with hot water. He probably thought Steve was going to boil him alive!

While helping him get ready Steve observed that John was wearing jeans and a shirt but no underwear. We gave him a pair. He looked quizzically at them but slipped them on, undoubtedly thinking that we had some pretty strange ideas.

Then it was time for bed. We pulled back the covers and encouraged John to climb in. Again he looked puzzled, and this time we understood why. Visiting his bedroom at the orphanage that afternoon we had seen that the beds were just slabs of wood without sheets or mattresses. The soft bed covered with fabric in which we were asking him to lie was quite outside his experience, but he cheerfully hopped in.

Over the next three days we spent a lot of time at the orphanage. As soon as we arrived each day cheerful children surrounded us, begging to have their picture taken. Each of them hoped that someday it would be their turn to leave with a family.

We met the English teacher and she put John and the other children through their paces. They recited lists of domesticated and wild animals (the camel was on the domesticated list) and named parts of their bodies. When the children recited the alphabet they said "zed" rather than "z", reflecting the British influence in India.

In the classroom the children sat on the floor. There were very few books and other school supplies. In fact, the coloring book we had sent John had been used by many children. Each child had carefully colored a page and signed his or her name. Something children in America take for granted was very cherished there.

One day we were chatting with the director in her office when a tiny newborn baby girl was brought in. Even though our son Peter had been born two months prematurely, this was by far the smallest child I had ever seen. "Why isn't she in an isolette in the hospital?" I gasped.

"It costs six American dollars per day to keep a baby in the hospital. We don't have that kind of money. We bring the abandoned babies here and do the best we can. Most survive, but some don't," Saila told me.

Other tiny babies were brought in, all girls. "Where are the boys?" we inquired.

"In India a girl is a liability because the family will have to pay a dowry for her," said Saila. "It's not hard to find an Indian family to adopt the baby boys, especially those with fair skin. But it's very hard to find someone to take a baby girl."

Steve and I were aghast. We wanted to gather all these precious little ones and bring them home with us, but of course that's not how the adoption process works. More than ever we were reminded that as Christians the value of women isn't questioned. The Lord ascribes equal value to male and female, Jew and Gentile, slave and free. In fact, men are told to honor women and lay down their lives for them. A person's worldview affects so much more than is apparent at first.

The day before we left Basundhara the orphanage threw a goodbye party for John. Saila gave each of us an Indian outfit. Steve and John dressed in their long white tunics and tight white cotton pants. Some of the older girls painted my toenails and feet red—not with nail polish, but with real paint! They helped me put on my beautiful navy and pink sari properly and escorted me to the party room. All the children crowded around again and begged for us to take their pictures. The orphanage social worker interviewed us while another worker videotaped us, asking why we wanted to adopt John. They hoped to share the tape with local authorities in hopes that they would feel more inclined to permit future adoptions.

The children sang some charming songs and some of the girls brought in a beautiful cake. It was so obvious that John had been loved at Basundhara. Each of his caregivers lovingly told him goodbye. His housemother struggled with tears as she hugged him, knowing he was going to have opportunities unavailable to him there but also knowing she would miss him so much. We promised to care for him well and assured them all that we would send pictures.

It was time to leave, but little Pupunu still grieved the loss of his friend. Again I knelt beside him, gave him a hug, and assured him that I would try to find a mommy for him. We knew it would be difficult, but we also knew that with God nothing is impossible.

We quickly hopped into the taxi and headed to the airport. For John, each new experience was exciting. Since everything we did was new to him, it was like being on a different planet. He was very courageous and cooperative. We felt like we had really struck gold.

The trip back to America was long, involving four different flights and lasting about thirty-eight hours. John was so excited to meet his new brothers and sisters that he couldn't sleep. At last, on the forty-five minute flight from Seattle to Spokane, he drifted off. When he awoke he was in a world he couldn't have imagined in his wildest dreams. I Corinthians 2:9 tells us "No eye has seen, no ear has heard, no mind has conceived what God has prepared for those who love him." We were reminded that the incredible differences between America and his experiences in India were tiny compared to the differences between our lives here on earth and all that awaits us in heaven.

Our other five children and many friends greeted us at the Spokane airport. John was delighted to meet each brother and sister and quite proud that he had learned their names. We eagerly drove home and showed him around the house.

John is able to see only outlines and shadows. We were amazed at how quickly he learned his way around the house and settled in. Extremely happy with all of his new experiences, each day John spontaneously yelled, "Yahoo!" several times. We were delighted with his quick adjustment.

One day as I swept the kitchen floor I found several small pieces of torn wallpaper on the ground. Investigating, I saw that strips had been pulled off the walls in several places. Calling all of the children together I asked them what was going on. They all denied any knowledge of the wallpaper situation. I decided to keep my eye on John, and it wasn't long until he raced upstairs, rounded the corner into the kitchen, and pulled off some wallpaper as he left the room.

Steve and I showed John the torn paper and tried to explain to him that the walls were supposed to look pretty. It was hard for him to understand, but he agreed he would leave the walls alone.

A few days later I went outside on the deck to have my morning devotions. I sat in the pretty wicker furniture Steve had given me a few years earlier. I always cherished the quiet moments before everyone else was up and the rush of the day began. As I opened my Bible I glanced at the ground and saw little pieces of wicker strewn all around. Appalled, I saw that several pieces of furniture had been picked at. The culprit was obviously John.

When the children awoke I called the older ones together and instructed them to be on fidget patrol. Clearly John didn't understand about keeping things nice. Additionally, we were beginning to learn that it is easy for a person with severe vision loss to retreat into his own world and not really think about what he's doing. John would sit in a chair by the hour, rocking and staring, apparently doing nothing.

When I asked John to find something to do he had no idea where to start. Apparently he didn't know how to play with toys or do anything productive other than run around outside. We began to teach him how to use different toys and sporting goods, and I started giving him a choice between three activities. At first it was very difficult for him to choose, but when he discovered that if he didn't we would give him a chore he began to learn to entertain himself.

John started third grade, in the same class with Deborah, and amazed everyone with his progress. His English skills exploded, he learned to read enlarged print and Braille, and he made friends easily. Within months he had endeared himself to everyone and proved that he was a tenacious, courageous child. His new life had begun, and we knew our lives would never be dull.

# CHAPTER 11

## Lessons from Abhilash

$\mathcal{B}$y the time we adopted John we were comfortable with the idea of building our family through adoption. We were eager to welcome another child into the group. Our biggest issue this time was deciding which child the Lord had planned for us.

It's overwhelming to consider all the children in the U.S. and around the world who need permanent, loving families and to recognize that only a small percentage will have them. We sometimes wonder why the Lord reached down His hand and, out of tens of thousands of needy children, chose to bless our children. It's a vivid illustration of Ephesians 1:4—"Just as He chose us in Him before the foundation of the world, that we should be holy and blameless before Him." We were chosen as the Lord's children without any merit on our part, and our children were chosen to be adopted apart from anything they did to earn a family.

As we desperately tried to know which child the Lord had planned for our family, we read Psalm 37:5—"Commit your way to the Lord, trust also in Him, and He will do it." We were confident that as we sought His direction He would make clear the child He had planned for us.

When we weren't allowed to adopt Pearl we gained confidence that the Lord was directing. Later, when we had to choose between Abhilash and Ganesh, we again saw Him at work as He placed one boy on Jim and Audry's heart and the other on our hearts.

Proverbs 3:5 and 6 says "Trust in the Lord with all your heart, and do not lean on your own understanding. In all your ways acknowledge Him, and He will make your paths straight." We saw that as we stepped out in faith the Lord directed our steps.

Lessons the Lord taught us through Abhilash:

- A strong appreciation for His choice of us as His children
- A willingness to daily commit our choices to Him
- A confidence that He would indeed direct us to a child that would fit into our family well

## JOHN TIMOTHY ABHILASH'S THOUGHTS ON HIS LIFE

John, age eleven, on top of a horse (and the world)

My name is John Timothy Abhilash Gardner and I'm eleven years old. I used to live in India with my birth mom and my brother. My birth dad died before I was born. My birth mother was very sick a lot so I would just go and wander around with nothing to do. My brother would play games with other kids. When my birth mother was very sick she took my brother and me to an orphanage in the mountains. The people at the orphanage wouldn't let my brother stay there because they thought he would run away. My birth mom left me there any way. I cried when she left. I think I was about six years old then.

Later Auntie Teri (from the adoption agency) came to the mountain orphanage and took me to the big orphanage at Basundhara. The first night I was scared, wondering what they were going to do to me. Then a nice boy named Bhanja became friends with me. When he left for America to be adopted I was sad. Then Pupunu came to Basundhara and he became my friend too. Pupunu and I were in the same room, and we played hide and go seek and slept in one bed together.

One day a man at Basundhara told me I would be adopted. Auntie Teri showed me pictures and gave me a shirt from my new parents. I thought it would be fun to see my dog and my new brothers and sisters. I wore the new shirt if we were taking nice pictures or going somewhere. My housemother wouldn't let me wear it other times.

Finally one day the man told me that my mom and dad were there to get me and I was happy. I walked outside to meet them and I was a little scared. My dad showed me an airplane and he showed me how to put it together and we played with the airplane for awhile. Then we went to the hotel and played with little cars. I love cars. The next day we went to buy some things for my brothers and sisters and we went back to Basundhara and played there. My mom and dad talked to Saila. She gave us nice Indian clothes. Mom and Dad bought me sandals and we had a going away party.

Then it was time to leave and I felt a little sad. I knew I would miss my friends a lot. But when we got to Spokane I was really happy to see my brothers and sisters at the airport. When we got home I played cars with my brothers and my sister Rebekah let our dog in the house and I was happy to see him. The dogs in India are mean but our dog is very nice.

My family is very nice and they take care of me. They help me find whatever I need. We do lots of fun things together. We went to family camp and I got to go down a really big slide. I also went on the high ropes course. It was scary but my dad helped me. We went to a ranch and I got to ride a horse by myself.

I like America because at school they really care about my sisters and me. They help me learn things. They gave me a special television at my desk that I can use to see my teacher at the front of the class. They have a Braille teacher for me. I like to play at school. I like soccer and music and P.E.. I go to chess club and sometimes I win.

I'm glad I'm in America because my mom and dad help me and take me to the doctor to help my eye. I'm glad I have a nice family and brothers and sisters and grandmas and grandpas and nice teachers.

I like to go to church and learn verses and learn about God. I know God loves me and He has a plan for me.

# CHAPTER 12

## Whatever happened to Pupunu?

As soon as we returned home from India with John we began telling everyone we knew about his little friend Pupunu. We had lot of pictures of him since he was always hanging around John, and several families were attracted to his sweet smile. His medical condition, however, was just too significant for any family to seriously consider adopting him.

One family got his medical records from the adoption agency and took them in to a blood specialist. The doctor was quite discouraging, telling them that raising such a child could destroy their marriage and their relationships with their other children. Given this information they felt they couldn't proceed.

One day we received a phone call from an acquaintance who attended our church's daughter church. Someone had told her about Pupunu and she wanted more information. She and her husband already had three birth children but had begun feeling the pull to adopt. They hadn't considered a child with physical challenges, but Mary was intrigued when she learned about Pupunu.

I told her all I knew and she shared the information with her husband, Scott. Although he was willing to adopt, he couldn't believe that Mary was suggesting they consider such a needy child. He believed that it would be too great a stress on their family.

A few weeks later our family and the Segallas attended a family camp hosted by our two churches. It was a fun weekend with lots of activity. Our son John had only been with us two months and he had the time of his life playing on a gigantic slide, conquering the high ropes course and canoeing on the river. Deborah was seldom far from John's side as they went on adventures together.

All weekend Scott watched the children, seeing how capable and happy they were and noting the joy they brought to our family. When camp was over he told Mary he'd changed his mind— she could find out what they needed to do to adopt Pupunu. He had decided that it wouldn't be so scary to adopt a child with physical challenges after all.

With delight Mary went to talk to the same blood specialist the other family had consulted. At first he tried to dissuade her, but soon he saw that her mind was made up. She wasn't trying to decide whether they should adopt Pupunu but merely wanted information on what would be involved in raising him, since the decision had already been made. Once he realized they were committed to adopting Pupunu the doctor's attitude changed completely and he became very supportive of Scott and Mary and carefully explained all the medical details.

The Segallas quickly began the paperwork process and just a year after John had arrived in America Pupunu, now Joey, joined his new family. His brothers and sister fell in love with him immediately and his quick wit and cheerful personality have been a delight.

A couple of days after his arrival I called to talk with him. I could barely understand him as he chattered away cheerfully in a mixture of English and his Indian language. Then I said, "Joey, this is John's mom. I met you in India when we came to get him. I told you that I would try to find a mommy for you. Do you remember that?"

Joey was quiet for a moment, and then in the sweetest voice imaginable he said, "Yes. Thank you for my mommy."

Joey has adapted extremely well to his new family and his life in the States. He and John get together regularly to play. Most exciting of all is his medical prognosis. With the care available here his life expectancy may be thirty or even forty years, compared to twelve in India.

Things have gone so well that the Segallas are now pursuing the adoption of a little two year old girl from John and Joey's orphanage who has vision like John's. We are all eagerly looking forward to her arrival several months from now.

# CHAPTER 13

## The Blessings of Adoption

*A*s we welcome precious children into our families, love them, meet their needs and help them learn to love the Lord, we should see a number of results.

### The Blessing of Raising Children

The most obvious blessing, of course, is that we have the privilege of raising a child or children and the great pleasure of seeing them learn, grow, and thrive. It is obvious but truly remarkable nevertheless to see the changes that occur in a child over the years and to know we were a catalyst for many of those changes. Of course childrearing takes lots of time, a large financial and emotional commitment, and a great deal of patience, but raising godly leaders for the next generation is certainly worth every effort.

Of course, raising kids is a lot of fun, too. We often watch our kids as they interact together and comment, "What did we do for entertainment before they came along?" The bond of parenting can draw a couple together in a special way as they enjoy experiences with their growing children.

## The Blessing of Seeing New Birth in our Children

A few months after we adopted Deborah some friends offered our family frequent flyer miles to travel to Singapore from our home in Taiwan for spring vacation. (Ahh, it's a rough life, being a missionary!) When we checked in for our flight we were shocked to discover that our seats were in first class! We settled into the extremely comfortable surroundings and wished the flight would last longer than four hours.

Once we were traveling I looked around at my children and mused at the remarkable providence of the Lord in their lives. My three birth children were having the adventure of their lives and it was fun to see. But it was the situation of our adopted children that really touched me. Just months earlier they had lived in bleak orphanages, quite literally without any hope for the future. Now as members of our family they were riding high in first class, on their way to Singapore, which is certainly one of the most beautiful cities in the world, with flight attendants at their beck and call. It was a beautiful picture of what happens to us when we become members of the family of God—we are taken out of the kingdom of darkness and enter the kingdom of His beloved Son (Col. 1:13). Watching this happen in the lives of our children is one of life's greatest joys.

## The Blessing of Being Able to Share about our Adoption as Believers

When families adopt a child of another ethnic group, it draws attention to their family. We have discovered that the countrymen of our children are quite curious as to why we adopted them. When we lived in Taiwan Rebekah was hospitalized for surgery on her cleft palate. Adoption is not common in Taiwan, and the nurses wanted to know why we had adopted her. Their first assumption was that we hadn't been able to have children, but when our other three children came to visit they realized that wasn't the case. When they asked me why we adopted her, I replied that it was because we loved her. They probed further and said that since we didn't know her before we met and adopted her we couldn't have known we would love her.

I then had the wonderful opportunity to share with them that we loved her just the way she was, even before we met her, and that God loves us just the way we are. We don't have to change anything to be accepted into His family. (Of course, when we are in His family we will want to change!) Rebekah didn't have to meet any criteria to be accepted into our family, but now that she was in our family she would probably begin acting in "Gardner family" ways, just as new believers begin to be conformed to the image of Christ.

The nurses were very intrigued. It was a new concept to be loved by God just as they are. Their religious traditions have taught them that they have to earn favor with the gods and that in fact they can never know if their good deeds outweigh their bad deeds, so can't be assured of salvation. What a blessing to be able to open their eyes to the love of the true God through the life of an adopted child.

We have seen similar reactions from Russians and Indians as they realize we have adopted a child from their country. Because Deborah and John both have very noticeable physical handicaps, Russians and Indians have been quite interested in our motivation for adopting these children. We have had many opportunities to share our faith in the Lord as a result of this.

Families involved in domestic adoptions will have similar opportunities to share their faith and motivation, as all adoptions are a picture of the believer's adoption into the Lord's family.

## The Blessing of Watching a Chain Reaction of Adoption

When we adopted for the first time, we didn't know anyone else who had adopted internationally or who had adopted an older child. We had no support group and no one with whom to discuss procedures or adoption issues. Because we lived overseas we weren't even able to talk with representatives from our adoption agency easily (this was before the easy accessibility of e-mail!) We simply started out on our own, learned as we went, bumbled along and made a lot of mistakes and yet somehow were totally blessed by the Lord with a wonderful daughter.

Friends watched us throughout this process. Within three years of Rebekah's adoption, at least six other families adopted as a direct result of observing the process. It seems like somebody had to go first, to lead the way and show it could successfully be done. This chain reaction has been delightful to observe, making us feel like we've had a part in impacting the lives of many children and families.

In churches a similar phenomenon can occur as families see how well adoptions can work. Often someone has to be first, and then they can use their experience to help others.

## The Blessing of Enjoying Diverse Cultural Experiences

One thoroughly delightful aspect of being a member of a family made up of many cultures has been the opportunity to be welcomed into various ethnic communities. We have been invited to participate in activities put on by Chinese, Russian and Indian groups and our personal lives have been so enriched. Our home is decorated diversely—we have the Chinese room, the Russian area, the Indian area, and even the African room, from when we spent a year in Ivory Coast as missionaries. Our children never lack items to share for show and tell!

This ethnic diversity has helped our children have a very real heart for the lost and be very missions minded. We regularly discuss newspaper articles about the countries our children are from and encourage pride in their heritage. Deborah particularly is proud of her heritage and when she hears a radio news item will shout out, "That's my Russia!"

During the 2000 summer Olympics we saw the hearts of our children as they cheered for athletes from their birth countries. Our Chinese daughter in particular was totally supportive of the Chinese women's gymnastics team. Being a gymnast herself, she watched each event with delight. When the Chinese team performed exceptionally well Rebekah claimed, "I'm not American! I'm Chinese!" We assured her she is both, and although she is proud to be an American at that time her allegiance was definitely with the Chinese.

We truly desire that all of our children, whether they were adopted or not, will feel an affinity for various people groups of the world and pour their lives' energies and resources into making a difference for eternity wherever the Lord might lead them.

# CHAPTER 14

# The Heir, the Spare, and the Little Princess Share Their Thoughts

**P**eter's thoughts—When I reflect on the past eight years, it is amazing to think that, once upon a time, adoption was not even a household term for us. So much has happened in eight short years. Three siblings have been added to our family's roster. With these additions came blood, sweat, and tears. The blood is in reference to the various squabbles that any "veteran" brother or sister will get into with a "rookie". Our family experienced our share of those. I remember that Deborah would shake her little stubs at us whenever she was angry, and say "Duna!" (the Russian equivalent of stupid). Quickly she learned that this was not acceptable, and we all are amazed at how much she has changed.

To facilitate change requires sweat. This sweat was poured out by every person in our family as we worked to teach our siblings English. We also had to work at teaching them skills that every American should know. I remember going with John to the nearby elementary school, pushing his bike. Countless hours and many scrapes later, my blind brother could ride a bike . . . without training wheels. Needless to say, I felt proud that I could have taught him this.

If anyone should feel proud, however, it is the kids themselves. They've worked so hard at becoming "one of us". They are always happy. Deborah and John, despite their tremendous obstacles, never complain. In fact, John runs through the house yelling, "Today is a yahoo day!!" It really puts me in my place. I have so much compared to them. My potential is so great. Am I using it? Am I complaining about trivial things?

As I write this and reflect, it almost makes me shed tears of joy to remember all the great memories I've shared with my great family. These moments would never have existed if it were not for Rebekah, Deborah, and John. They add so much spice to life.

Though I've tried, I have never been able to imagine life without these three great individuals. Not only are they my siblings, but they are my heroes. I feel honored to be a part of their lives. Through the blood, the sweat, and the tears, we have made a family. But are we even done? Who else might God decide to place in our paths? I can not wait to find out.

**Aaron's thoughts** - To say that I have always been perfectly accepting of the concept of adoption would be untrue. I was undoubtedly the one biological child of our family who had serious doubts about the entire adoption process. Up until I was nine years old, before we brought any new children into our family, I already considered it complete. Two parents, two sons, a daughter, a dog—what more did we need? Never in my wildest dreams did I imagine that one day we would have twice as many children. At that early stage in my life it would have been almost unfathomable to my young mind.

The day my parents told us about the prospect of adopting Rebekah, Peter and Susannah immediately embraced the idea. I was quite reticent in my personal opinions, but decided that I would go along with whatever my family decided. Why my parents felt the need to bring a complete stranger into our lives was beyond me. But the family chose to adopt Rebekah, and that was that.

Many long months later, Peter, Susannah, and I drove to the airport along with our dad, to welcome our mother and the new arrival from China. My dad had come back from China early in order to continue at his job. We met the two eagerly, and from that point on Rebekah was one of us. I learned very early on that she was not going to be treated like a little princess while our parents forgot about the rest of the kids. She was an equal in every aspect of life. Though it took some adjusting, within a short time we all came to love her, even me.

I still remember vividly the moment when my mom told me about Deborah. After an unusually boring day of school, I played a pickup game of basketball with some buddies on a court within the campus. Gradually each boy's mom or dad came to collect him, as did my mother. As we chatted away, one of my favorite pastimes, she mentioned that she and my dad were considering the possibility of adopting another girl. Trying to stay optimistic, I posed various questions, such as the child's age, country of origin, and so forth. At some point in the conversation my mom told me that the girl had been born without arms. I was aghast. In a not so calm manner, I informed my mother that adopting a girl with a fixable cleft palate was one thing, but adopting one without arms was completely different. She told me right back that she and dad had not decided yet, but were prayerfully considering it, to see if it was the Lord's will. *Great,* I thought, *now she has to drag God into*

135

*this*. That quieted my protests, and once again I determined that my parents knew what was best.

Another great span of time later, my parents arrived at the airport with my new sister. The moment I laid eyes upon her, I knew that she was a Gardner. With her adorable face, witty humor and never-ending smile, it was impossible not to accept her. Her lack of hands proved to be not nearly as serious as I originally assumed. Deborah can eat, write, draw, and do countless other tasks with the single digit she has on each stub, and whatever she can't do with them, she can do with her feet. Recently croqueting has become one of Deborah's hobbies, just another example of how God has made her able to do the things that "normal" people love.

By the time that John became a possibility, I knew that nothing I said or did would change the Lord's plan for our family. Though in my lack of faith I couldn't imagine having a mostly blind brother, I was a little more willing to accept him than I had been with Rebekah and Deborah. At fifteen, I had never had a little brother, and was eager to teach him the skills that I knew. Peter and I, being only two years apart, learned nearly every sport at the same time. In John, I had a kid to teach to throw a football, shoot a basketball, or run in a race. Between Peter and me, we have taught John the traditional American pastimes, and he has shown to be promising in many of them. At times I even forget that he is for the most part blind. Though a little quiet, he adds a new element to our family, and I couldn't imagine him not being in it.

Though I have been in a way the "Doubting Thomas" in our family when it comes to adoption, God has shown me that new children can truly be a blessing. Through the years He has challenged my lack of faith, and encouraged and strengthened my trust in Him as a result. Without the three adopted children, we would not be a complete family. Each of them is dear to me, and I would not wish for life without them.

**Susannah's thoughts** - I was six years old when my parents adopted Rebekah. I was so excited because I really wanted a little sister. Through the entire adoption process I was very impatient to get my new sister. The day finally came when my parents left to get Rebekah. My grandmother was staying with my brothers and me. I'm sure I was quite a pest the entire time my parents were gone. When Rebekah and my mom got home after a few weeks in China (my dad had to come home sooner to work) I was finally happy. I now had my little sister.

A year passed and I was fine growing up with two brothers whom I loved and now a little sister who I could play with and grow up with. Then one day my brother Peter went and talked to my mom. She was doing the dishes and I was helping and he said something like this, "Mom, I found this girl in our adoption magazine and I want you and dad to think about adopting her. Before you see her picture I just want to tell you I think she would be a great help around the house and a great sister to Susannah and Rebekah."

My mom called my dad into the room and Peter showed them a picture of the most beautiful East Indian girl ever. She was 13 and he was 12. My parents said they really didn't think she would be good in our family which I was glad about because I didn't want an older sister. Then Peter said he had been joking and he actually wanted them to adopt the girl whose picture was under the other girl's. I looked at the picture and immediately fell in love with that little girl. I guess my parents didn't quite have the same reaction an eight year old had. They told Peter they didn't think it would be a good idea but he asked them to pray about it and they did. After a long time they told us we were getting Deborah.

Again I was excited to get a little sister. I adored my role as big sister a lot. My grandmother couldn't come stay with the left behind four when my parents went to Russia so a college girl from her church came to Taiwan to stay with us. I wasn't such a pest this time because I knew what to expect. The wait was still long and I really missed my parents but I wanted another little sister. Deborah finally came home and again our family was complete.

After we had moved back to America my parents somehow got the idea to adopt a little girl from Thailand. I was ecstatic at the thought of another little sister!!! But I guess God didn't want us to adopt Pearl because the Thailand government told us we had too many kids to adopt from there. I was really sad because I had grown to love this little girl like a sister even though I had never met her. I wondered why God didn't want us to get her but then I found out why.

A few months later I found out that my parents were considering adopting a little boy from India who was almost completely blind. At first I didn't know if I really wanted to because a blind boy might be kind of hard to take care of. I was much older this adoption, twelve in fact, and didn't have the little girl feeling of "I'm just getting another playmate" that I had in the other adoptions. I now actually thought about how my family would be able to help this child. I decided that it was God who wanted us to get this child because if we had adopted Pearl we would still be in the process and would never have even considered adopting this boy. I also thought we'd be able to help him because we had already adopted a girl with a cleft palate and a girl without arms. My parents and siblings felt the same way and we decided to adopt John.

My parents went to India to get John and now it was just days before I'd have a little brother to love. I knew he would fit in the family fine and, of course, when he came he did fit in. Again my family is complete, but maybe someday someone else will come into my family and complete us again. I wouldn't mind that at all.

# CHAPTER 15

## The Children Today

⁂

*I*t's the beginning of 2003 and life is a constant adventure. All six children are thriving. Peter is a freshman at Multnomah Bible College in Portland, Oregon. He is majoring in Communication and Bible and hopes that there might be a position for him with Kingdom Kids when he graduates. Since we have no paid employees at this point the ministry will have to grow a lot in the next three years, but we would be delighted if the Lord blessed in that way.

Peter has been one of the driving forces for our adoptions. Deborah knows that it was because of Peter that we pursued her adoption. The two of them have a very special relationship. John admires Peter tremendously and struggled greatly when Peter left for college. Steve took him to visit the school so that he could understand better what Peter is doing. Christmas vacation has been a wonderful time for the boys to renew their relationship. With all the wrestling and laughter that's gone on here the last three weeks it's surprising how few things have been broken!

Aaron is sixteen and a junior in high school. He is a tremendous help to us at the adoption conferences. He presents a very popular workshop entitled "How Adding Adopted Children to Your Family Affects your Birth Children." He is honest when he shares that we have less time and money for the older children due to expanding our family, but acknowledges that he wouldn't want life to be different.

Aaron encouraged me significantly recently. We were discussing what he should look for in a wife, and after mentioning his desire that she have a good sense of humor, love the Lord, and be reasonably pretty, he stated that she had to want to adopt. I was very surprised. "Sure, Mom," he said. "All of the kids plan to adopt." Not having heard this before I quickly assembled all the children. Most of them indicated that they plan to have biological children as well, but they all agreed that adoption is in their plans.

"You've shown us how many children need families and how important it is for us to help," they said. "We're not going to forget that when we have our own families." Steve and I were thrilled to learn that, not only do the children not feel that we have ruined their lives by adopting, but they recognize the blessings adoption brings to a family.

Susannah is fourteen and finishing eighth grade. Her experiences with her siblings have greatly influenced her life goals. When Deborah had weekly occupational therapy visits Susannah went along and learned to help out. Now she wants to be an occupational therapist and is beginning to work on her volunteer hours. After seeing pictures and videos of our trip to India, Susannah longs to use her occupational therapy skills there someday. Unlike in America, many children in India still deal with polio and

142

other challenges. There will be ample opportunities there for Susannah.

Susannah's friends often visit our house. All of them are from small families, with only one brother or sister. They comment wistfully that there is always something going on at our house, and that their homes seem boring by comparison. They also seem envious of the sweet relationships Susannah has with her younger sisters and brother. She is very kind and helpful to them and a genuine blessing to me.

Last Christmas was John's first Christmas ever. We knew that the whole holiday season would be overwhelming to him, so decided that we would simplify things as much as possible. With very little urging on our part, the older children agreed that it would be a good idea to only have one present for each child. They willingly contacted their relatives and asked them to send money rather than presents. Then they looked through a Partners International catalog and selected gifts for people around the world with the money. Peter's money enabled a family in Cambodia to start a small business. Aaron's money paid for a well in India. Susannah bought a couple of piglets for a family in Vietnam. Rebekah bought Bibles for China, Deborah bought a bike for a farmer, and John bought Bibles for India.

Steve and I made a special gift for each child. Because we knew that it wouldn't take long to unwrap one gift each, we took a ball of yarn for each child and unwound it throughout the house, garage and yard. At the end of the ball was the child's gift. The children had so much fun winding the yarn into balls and finding their gifts, playing games and visiting children at a local hospital that they told us it was their best Christmas ever. Again we were blessed with our children's willingness to be flexible and look out for the interests of others.

Rebekah is thirteen now and has made tremendous strides in her time in our family. School has never been easy for her but she works very hard. Apparently she wasn't spoken to very much in her orphanage and her language skills were quite underdeveloped when we adopted her at age five. We have been told that if a child doesn't learn a language—any language—by the time she is three or four the parts of the brain for language learning begin to atrophy. Language has been a challenge for Rebekah. Years of speech and language therapy have helped to a degree but she will probably always need to work hard.

Rebekah and I spent many weeks together in hospitals as she had six surgeries to repair her clefts. One final surgery this summer will repair her nose so that she will have fewer nosebleeds.

Rebekah is a loving, sweet young lady who enjoys gymnastics, swimming and horseback riding. Because school has been a challenge for her we have tried to find other activities at which she can excel. Her tiny little body makes her a natural for these events.

Deborah is ten years old and an inspiration to everyone she meets. She accepts herself the way the Lord made her. As we were driving to church one day she asked if she would have long arms in heaven. Steve assured her that she would. She replied, "Oh, I would really miss my short arms!"

She has had five surgeries because as she grows the bones in her stubs grow and the skin and tissue around them doesn't grow enough, which could ultimately result in the bones poking through the skin. It becomes quite painful, so the surgeon cuts off part of the bone and all is well for several months, until the bones grow enough to bother her again and it's time to do it over. This will probably continue until she finishes growing. We have found Shriner's Hospital for Crippled Children to be extremely child-friendly. Each time Deborah is hospitalized it is a very positive experience for her as she observes other children with orthopedic problems, many of them far worse than hers. It's a good reminder that other children have struggles, too.

Deborah tried a prosthetic arm several years ago, but quickly found that it really wasn't any help. It was bulky and cumbersome, had no sensation, and she could only move the "elbow" by maneuvering it with her knee. She told us that she didn't need it because she could already do everything without it. We agreed and she hadn't asked about prosthetics again.

Then, at her regular clinic visit a few months ago, Deborah asked her doctor if she could have artificial arms that would look like real arms, even though they wouldn't be useful to her. She thought wearing them at the mall and other public places would lessen the number of stares and occasional rude remarks with which she has to deal.

The doctor said he thought they could come up with something and made an appointment for her a month in the future. A week before the appointment Deborah asked me to cancel it. When I asked why she said, "If the arms would help me it would be different, but since they won't I don't think that I should try to hide the way that God made me." I assured her that if she ever changed her mind I would reschedule the appointment, but she seemed to have a new peace after that.

Deborah attends regular public school and functions very well in the classroom. She has many friends and we are delighted when we see the children play games, the other girls using their hands while Deborah uses her feet. We feel it is a positive experience for the other children to have Deb in their classroom. They assist her with small tasks such as carrying her full lunch tray or zipping her winter jacket. It opens their world a bit.

John is eleven years old and absolutely thriving. We are extremely grateful to the staff at our local elementary school. They have gone so far beyond what was required of them to meet John's needs. In just a year and a half they have gotten him reading at a third grade level, taught him Braille, helped him learn all his math facts, and expanded his world.

After appointments with several eye surgeons we realized that there is nothing that can be done to improve John's vision, at least at this point. But we are constantly amazed at all he can do. He loves to play soccer and chess. He has learned to ride a bike and doesn't understand why we won't let him ride it off down the street! I tell him that he won't see a car and it will hit him, but he's skeptical. We let him ride at the school playground and it's his favorite pastime.

John and Deborah are best friends. We have a small orchard, and each fall we need to send the children out to gather the apples that have fallen on the ground. John and Deb work together. Without arms, it's difficult for Deb to pick up the apples. She spots one and points to it with her foot. John follows her foot and picks up the apple. It is a wonderful example of the body of Christ working together.

Certainly all six children have their moments of being selfish and uncooperative, but generally those times are rare. We feel the Lord has blessed us beyond our wildest dreams with the privilege of having a part in the development of each of their lives. They certainly are a heritage from the Lord, and we believe that our adoption adventures have had a significant part in molding their characters.

## Susannah, Aaron, Peter, Deborah, John, and Rebekah–Summer 2002

Recently we received our foster parenting license, and we are eagerly awaiting a new adventure as we anticipate having another child in our home. We have requested a long term placement of a physically challenged child and hope to hear about a child soon. It's exciting to anticipate the joy another little one will bring to our family.

# Conclusion

*A*bba, Father! Of all the pictures the Lord uses to describe His relationship with believers, that of a loving father to adopted children is perhaps the most tender. As the body of Christ observes families who have lovingly welcomed adopted children into their midst, we gain a much greater appreciation of our own adoption into the family of God.

May the Lord give you wisdom as He shows you how you and your church can be a part of making a difference for eternity in the life of a child.

"Do not withhold good from those who deserve it, when it is in your power to act." Proverbs 3:27

# The Story of Kingdom Kids Adoption Ministries

After each of our adoptions our friends asked many questions about the process. They were curious about how we had integrated our birth children with our adopted children, what it was like to adopt older kids with physical challenges, what was involved in the process, and many other things. We realized that there was a great need for information.

The more we saw how well each of our children adjusted and how much fun we had as we expanded our family, the more we wanted to encourage other families to consider adoption.

We wanted to provide a means for families to get their questions about adoption answered in one place and also to provide support for families who had already adopted. We had already established Kingdom Kids Foundation when we were raising money for John's adoption. Now we wanted not only to help other families raise finances for their adoptions, but also to encourage, educate and equip the body of Christ to pursue adoption as a ministry.

As we considered the best method to do this, we felt it was important that we not be an adoption agency. We wanted to be a neutral entity, able to listen to each family's situation and point them toward agencies that might be able to help them.

I rounded up a group of friends interested in adoption and we decided to hold a large conference in Spokane to provide information and support to families interested in adoption. We contacted all the adoption agencies in Washington and Idaho and invited them to participate. The response overwhelmed us as twenty-three groups signed up to display. Most of the groups also agreed to present workshops on different adoption topics. We began advertising this full day event to the community, not knowing what kind of reaction to expect.

The response showed us that there is a definite need for adoption information to be presented from a Biblical perspective in an accessible way. Nearly three hundred people attended that first conference in November of 2001, visiting the agency displays, listening to keynote speakers and attending forty different workshops. Over the next several months we heard from many of the people who attended the conference, telling us it had given them the information and encouragement they needed to actually pursue an adoption.

That was the incentive we needed to encourage us to present more conferences. We applied to the Internal Revenue Service for 501(c)(3) non-profit status and were delighted when, after completing pages and pages of paperwork, it was granted. We incorporated as Kingdom Kids Adoption Ministries and held four more conferences in 2002, one each in Seattle, Portland, San Jose and Spokane. Another adoptive family, Greg and Terri Bade and their five children, joined our ministry team and helped present the conferences.

Each conference taught us lessons about how to do the next one better. We kept hearing back from people who had attended, letting us know of their adoption plans. It was both exhilarating and tiring as we learned as we went.

Our third conference was held in May, 2002, in Portland, Oregon. The attendance was excellent, mostly couples at the beginning stages of considering adoption. They were eager learners and plied the workshop presenters with questions. At the end of the busy weekend we knew many lives would be changed as a result of the event.

However, we also realized that we had lost money on each conference we had presented and were out of funds to continue the ministry. Because advertising on Christian radio seems to be the most effective method of letting people know about the conferences, and because radio advertising is expensive, we weren't breaking even on the conferences. The fees we charged the displayers and the attendees were minimal and simply weren't covering the expenses. Yet we didn't want to charge any more for fear that it would keep away the very people to whom we wanted to minister.

As we drove back to Spokane from Portland I felt a mixture of frustration and sadness. We had eagerly begun Kingdom Kids and saw the Lord blessing many lives as a result. We had spent our savings and had no more to invest. Apparently this was the end of the Kingdom Kids conferences. Much as I racked my brain I couldn't think of realistic alternative funding possibilities.

We arrived home late Saturday night. On Sunday afternoon one of the children ran to tell me that a fax was arriving. I wasn't expecting anything, so curiously tore it from the machine. It was from the same Chinese friend in Taiwan who had paid for our flight to Russia to adopt Deborah and contributed so heavily to John's adoption expenses. She was interested in what we were doing through Kingdom Kids and said that she wanted to deposit some money in our bank account but needed our account number. We were surprised to hear from her. It was a remarkable answer to prayer that she would contact us right when we were feeling that our resources were exhausted and we would need to quit presenting the conferences.

We had no idea how much money she intended to deposit, but several days later we received a notice from our bank that a large deposit had been made. It was enough to enable us to put on four more conferences as well as hire a grant writer, produce a professional video, and move the ministry out of our home into a small downtown office. The timing of her generous gift gave us confidence that the Lord wasn't ready for us to give up on Kingdom Kids. With eager hearts we have not only continued the ministry but also been able to expand it in several ways.

Kingdom Kids Adoption Ministries exists to impact eternity by encouraging the body of Christ to embrace adoption and support adoptive families. Our ministries include:

o   Educating the community of believers about adoption issues.

   -   Providing speakers about adoption issues for church events.

- Providing written materials for children's workers so they can understand the issues adopted children in their ministry may face.

o Encouraging, educating and equipping adoptive and foster families through conferences, support groups and networking.

- Presenting informational conferences for adoptive and pre-adoptive families with keynote speakers, workshops and agency displays.
- Facilitating the formation of area support groups.
- Providing well-researched printed resources and materials.

o Encouraging families to consider adoption, especially of waiting children.

- Connecting interested families with adoptive families who are willing to answer questions.
- Disseminating information about adoption and referring to appropriate agencies.
- Providing families with information on waiting children.

o Educating Crisis Pregnancy Center workers regarding adoption as a positive option for their clients.

- Providing a special track of workshops at our conferences designed for CPC workers to learn how to communicate about adoption with women in unplanned pregnancies.

- Providing speakers for training at individual Crisis Pregnancy Centers.

o   Equipping families to finance adoption.

- Assisting families in contacting friends to encourage tax-deductible donations for adoptions.
- Referring families to other organizations that can provide financial help.

o   As the Lord provides resources, our future ministries will include:

- Presenting sanctity of life seminars in Russia in order to encourage believers there to minister to physically handicapped children in need of adoption.
- Expanding adoption conferences across the country to educate believers about this vital need and their opportunity to impact a child for eternity.
- Following up on families after they have adopted, to refer them to support groups and other resources they may need.
- Writing and publishing additional materials to educate the body of Christ about adoption issues.

The possibilities are limited only by time and money. As interested people volunteer to help with the ministry and support Kingdom Kids financially, we will be able to challenge more and more families to consider making a difference for eternity in the life of a child.

Kingdom Kids depends on the generous support of interested friends to allow us to continue this ministry.

In 2003 we anticipate presenting six conferences, one each in Seattle, Portland, Spokane, Phoenix, Detroit, and California. We also hope to partner with other groups and become a vital force in the Christian community.

# *How to Get Started in Adoption*

*I*f after reading this you think the Lord might be nudging you to consider adoption, there are several things you can do to get started. There is no one correct way to begin, but these are some ideas.

1. **Do research.** Talk with families who have already adopted. Attend conferences and trainings. Look on the internet. Keep your options open at the beginning–consider domestic, international and foster adoption.

2. **Questions you'll need to consider:**

   o *Our readiness to adopt*:

      - Are we willing to change our lifestyle to accommodate a child?
      - Do we enjoy children and parenting?
      - Are we patient and do we have a sense of humor, or are we rigid and judgmental?

- Are we willing to travel a road other people may not understand?
- If we have dealt with infertility, are we ready to move on?
- Are we in agreement that adoption is right for our family?

o *The type of adoption best for us*:

- How important is it to us that our child look like us?
- How long are we willing to wait to have a child placed in our home?
- With what age of child are we comfortable?
- Would we consider siblings?
- What are our financial resources?
- What physical/mental/emotional challenges do we believe we could handle?
- Which ones would absolutely be too difficult for us?
- Are we willing to integrate different cultural and ethnic backgrounds into our family?

3. **Determine whether domestic or international adoption is right for you.** You might contact agencies that handle both types of adoptions and ask them for information so you can compare programs and costs.

4. **Take preliminary steps.** If you have decided that you want to adopt internationally there are some things you can do prior to selecting an agency. This gives you time to research agencies while your paperwork is beginning to be processed.

o **Complete the INS application.** You need to get permission from the U.S. government to adopt a child from overseas and have the child immigrate to the United States. You can order the I-600A form, called the "Application for Advance Processing of Orphan Petition", from the INS or download it from their website.

o **Contract for a homestudy.** You need to contact a social worker to begin your home study, which is required for all adoptions, international or domestic. The agency you use for your adoption does not need to be the same agency that does your homestudy. To find out who does homestudies in your area, look in the yellow pages of the phone book under Adoption.

5. **Choose an agency.** If you haven't already done so, you need to select an agency at this point. This is a major decision. You are hiring this agency to help fulfill your dream of adopting a child.

Ways to find agencies in your area:

- Look in the Yellow Pages of the phone book under Adoption.
- Do a web search, entering "Washington Adoption Agencies" (substituting the name of your state.)
- Ask adoptive parents what agency they used and whether or not they were satisfied.
- Call Kingdom Kids (509-465-3520) for a list of agencies we have worked with and can recommend.

Remember that many agencies work nation-wide, and may not be listed specifically for your state.

6. **Complete the application to your chosen agency**. This is the way to commit yourself to working with a particular group. Once you have applied to the agency they will begin to work for you.

7. **Begin to prepare your dossier**. International adoptions require you to prepare a dossier that will be submitted to the foreign officials who will ultimately approve the adoption.

8. **Complete your dossier and await a child referral**. The time between dossier completion and receiving a referral varies between countries. For domestic adoptions, regional and national adoption exchanges publish photolisting books.

9. **Accept or reject the child referral**. Normally your referral will be very close to what you requested. Occasionally families are asked to consider a child a bit older or younger than they requested, or with special needs they hadn't considered. Carefully consider whether or not you feel you can meet the needs of the child. The Lord may ask you to consider something you might not have normally. If you are presented with a challenge you hadn't considered, it is wise to talk with other families raising a child with a similar condition. You can also research the condition on the internet and contact groups that you locate. It's a good idea to take the child's medical report to your pediatrician for an opinion of the child's potential. Raising a child with special needs can be one of the most rewarding experiences of your life.

10. **Prepare to travel or have the child escorted home**. Most countries require that adoptive parents travel to the country to meet and adopt the child. A few countries allow children to be es-

corted home. In domestic adoptions, typically families travel to meet the new child.

11. **After receiving your child, complete post-adoption study**. Countries and adoption agencies want to be sure the placement is successful for the family and that adoption is a good choice for children. It is very important that you cooperate with the post-adoption studies.

12. **Finalize the adoption**. In most countries the adoption is finalized overseas. In domestic adoptions and some international adoptions families must go through court hearings to legally complete the adoption. This usually takes place within six to twelve months of when the child is placed in your home.

Kingdom Kids has a three-ring binder **Adoption Planner** available with greater detail about each step of the adoption process. With questions to ask agencies and a format designed to help you keep all your information in one place, it is a useful tool to guide you through the process. Contact Kingdom Kids for ordering information.

Feel free to contact Kingdom Kids at any time with questions about adoption. We have many resources available to help you.

We can be reached at:

Kingdom Kids Adoption Ministries
8625 N. Whitehouse Dr.
Spokane, WA 99208
(509) 465-3520
kingdomkids@effectnet.com
www.kkadoption.com

To order additional copies of

*Adoption* as a Ministry,
Adoption as a *Blessing*

Have your credit card ready and call:

1-877-421-READ (7323)

or please visit our web site at
www.pleasantword.com

Also available at: www.amazon.com

Printed in the United States
9381000011B